The blue livery is much the same, but LNER A4 Pacific *Seagull*, sister to No. 4468 *Mallard*, which 11 years earlier set an all-time world steam railway speed record, departs from King's Cross in 1949, with its post-nationalisation British Railways' number 60033, and the name of the state railway on the tender.
F AYLARD/COLOUR-RAIL

THE NATION'S RAILWAY

70 years since the birth of British Railways January 1, 1948

COVER PICTURE: The first of Robert Riddles' 999 British Railways Standard steam locomotives, Class 7 Pacific No. 70000 *Britannia*, storms through Langcliffe on the Settle and Carlisle line on June 23, 2011. BRIAN SHARPE

PRODUCTION EDITOR:
Sarah Palmer

PAGE DESIGN:
Craig Lamb
Kriele Ltd
design_lamb@btinternet.com

COVER DESIGN:
Kelvin Clements

REPROGRAPHICS:
Paul Fincham
Jonathan Schofield

ADVERTISING:
Craig Amess
camess@mortons.co.uk

PUBLISHERS:
Steve O'Hara
Tim Hartley

PUBLISHING DIRECTOR:
Dan Savage

COMMERCIAL DIRECTOR:
Nigel Hole

MARKETING MANAGER:
Charlotte Park
cpark@mortons.co.uk

PRINTED BY:
William Gibbons and Sons,
Wolverhampton

ISBN:
978-1-911276-43-2

PUBLISHED BY:
Mortons Media Group Ltd,
Media Centre, Morton Way,
Horncastle, Lincolnshire
LN9 6JR.
Tel: 01507 529529

GWR 4-6-0 No. 4091 *Dudley Castle*, with British Railways on the tender side, at Chippenham in 1949. K LEITCH/COLOUR-RAIL

It's 70 years since the great watershed in Britain's railways. It was on January 1, 1948, that after an illustrious quarter of a century the Big Four companies; the Great Western, London Midland & Scottish, London & North Eastern and Southern railways passed into history, and the entire network came under state control on a permanent basis.

In both world wars, the government had, by necessity, taken overall control of the railways.

We habitually associate nationalisation – of any industry – as Labour party ideology, and indeed it was Clement Attlee's government, which was installed with a landslide general election victory in 1945, and went on to create British Railways.

However, it was a Conservative – and later Liberal prime minister – who first proposed the idea of the government running the nation's railways more than a century before, in the early years of Queen Victoria's reign, when the network was still taking shape, with several of the major trunk routes still to be built.

Historians look back at the years of post-Second World War austerity and many see that the government was at the time left with little option. Trains were still the country's predominant form of transport, both for passengers and freight, but years of neglect of maintenance and lack of investment during the conflict had left them seriously run down, at a crucial time when they were essential for the rebuilding of the nation.

The question has to be asked, and is still being asked today, is the government the right body to run the railway network, or should it be left to private enterprise with the benefits that competition promises?

From the outset, decisions were made according to available resources. The subsequent fortunes of Britain's railways might have been very different if the country had been able to follow the lead of the United States and other European countries in switching to diesel and electric traction much earlier than it did. Instead, lack of finance led to the steam era experiencing an Indian summer, with British Railways perpetuating the better Big Four designs before building a fleet of some of the finest steam locomotives any country had even seen, in Robert Riddles' 12 Standard classes.

Yet when modernisation came as austerity eased, it was a fudged affair, with a rush to embrace barely proven and sometimes inadequate diesel classes with the steam locomotive production lines still in full swing. Despite the fact that car ownership and road haulage were well into their ascendancy at the time when Prime Minister Harold Macmillan told us we had never had it so good, the nationalised railway was slow to respond to changing market conditions.

The disenfranchisement of many towns and rural communities by the steady closure of loss-making routes forced their residents to turn to motor transport. Replacement bus services were provided following closures, but often they proved inadequate and also ceased operation after a comparatively short time because they could not be made to pay.

Rail closures had been underway from the start of the British Railways' era, and gathered pace as the nationalised railways' debts soared to nightmarish proportions, leading to the appointment of business executive Dr Richard Beeching as chairman.

Beeching was quick to carve a reputation for himself as the most hated civil servant of all time, yet he was merely carrying out instructions from on high in Whitehall. He did not invent rail closures, but merely co-ordinated and streamlined the process by which they were carried out, in order to shape a vibrant inter-city network for the future, and one that we have, by and large, inherited today.

He did not, however, return British Railways to profitability, and taxpayers' subsidies have soared over the ensuing decades. In recent years, passenger numbers have reached an all-time high, and in 2016-17, the government subsidised the now-reprivatised network to the tune of £4.2 billion.

Indeed, a peak was reached in 2006-7, when government support for railways reached £7.5 billion. In autumn 2017, the

A year after Nationalisation, North British-built Jubilee 4-6-0 No. 5594 is still carrying its LMS livery and number as it heads through York. E SANDERSON/COLOUR-RAIL

Conservative government's Transport Secretary Chris Grayling announced that £48 billion would be spent on the network over a five-year period.

The Department for Transport has pointed out that the railways returned revenues to the taxpayer of around £763 million over the same period, and the Rail Delivery Group, said that private investment in rail reached a record level of £925 million in 2016-17.

The network still has its problems, not least of all long-running industrial disputes, which have at times paralysed services, and questions have been asked as to whether the government could, or should, have done more to improve the lot of passengers and keep fare increases in line with inflation.

The surprise resurgence of Labour under Jeremy Corbyn at the 2017 general election has placed the topic of rail nationalisation once again on the political agenda, asking whether its time has come again. But 2017 is not 1947: the privatised railway today has a very different structure to that of the Big Four era, and could Britain, once again emerging from years of austerity following the banking collapse of 2008, afford to buy out the private enterprises now running it?

One of the big mistakes of line closures under British Railways was the failure to see into the future beyond 30 years. Did Beeching, back in 1962, foresee a time when even families on low incomes would be two-car

households? The car may be undisputed king, but many now people choose the trains instead because of gridlocked roads in our big towns and cities, and the situation is getting worse.

Yes, there was little point in keeping lines open that few people used, but should the trackbeds have been protected from development so that they could once again be available for future use if needed?

From 1948 onwards, the running of British Railways was too often a learning curve, and if we seek to give the country the rail network that it needs and deserves, we must take on board the lessons of history as well as the requirements of the immediate times.

Bulleid Merchant Navy Pacific No. 35024 *East Asiatic Company* heads out of Waterloo in June 1949, the British Railways' motif on its tender side. S TOWNROE/COLOUR-RAIL

The long road to STATE OWNERSHIP

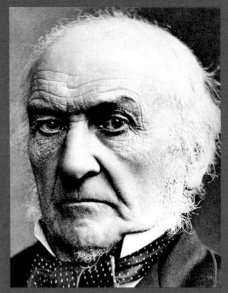

William Ewart Gladstone, who in 1844, threatened British railway companies with a state takeover if they did not cut fares for poorer sections of society.

January 1, 1948, is one of the seminal dates in British railway history, for it was then that the nation's railways merged under a single permanent owner – the nation. Yet the concept of nationalisation was by no means a Labour cure for a network worn out by six years of overwork and wartime austerity, for it had been mooted more than a century before, when many of our major routes had yet to be built.

Nationalisation of railways, or any industry for that matter, is commonly associated with socialist ideology, however, in Britain, the idea of bringing railways under state control began with one of the country's best-known Conservative and later Liberal politicians, namely William Ewart Gladstone.

Born on December 29, 1809 in Liverpool, the son of a prosperous merchant, Gladstone was educated at Eton and Oxford University and was elected to parliament in 1832, as a Conservative. He held junior offices in Robert Peel's government of 1834-35.

Despite the fact he was slowly moving towards Liberalism, he entered Peel's Conservative cabinet in 1843. When the Conservatives split in 1846, Gladstone followed Peel in becoming a Liberal-Conservative. However, between 1846 and 1859 Gladstone was politically isolated, although he held some cabinet posts, including Chancellor of the Exchequer.

In 1859, he joined the Liberals, becoming their leader in 1867 and the following year, prime minister for the first of four times.

A landslide defeat in the 1874 general election led to his arch-rival Benjamin Disraeli becoming Conservative prime minister, and Gladstone retired as Liberal leader.

However, Gladstone became prime minister for the second time in 1880, combining this with the office of chancellor for two years. He later served as prime minister in 1886 and 1892-94, after which he resigned because he was at odds with his Liberal cabinet.

He died from cancer on May 19, 1898 and was buried in Westminster Abbey.

What concerns us here, however, was the bill that Gladstone introduced into the House of Commons in 1844, when he was a Conservative Free Trader and president of the Board of Trade.

The Railway Regulation Act 1844, or to give it its correct title 'an Act to attach certain Conditions to the construction of future Railways authorised by any Act of the present or succeeding sessions of Parliament; and for other Purposes in relation to Railways' was the first piece of legislation that gave the British government the power to take over the nation's railways... half a century before the Labour Party was born or the railways' greatest rival, motor road transport, had emerged.

The concept of nationalisation, however, was not the brainchild of Gladstone. In 1843, in his book Railway Reform: Its Importance And Practicability, Considered As Affecting The Nation, The Shareholders And The Government, author William Galt discussed the potential for state purchase of the railways, and it was his idea that prompted Gladstone to include the potential for such a measure in his bill.

Galt compared Britain's railways with those in Belgium, and argued that the boom in railway building in the UK had led to waste of resources. He cited Belgium, where main lines linking principal cities had been built and run by the state. Looking at the average cost of building 71 railways in Britain,

The seeds of Nationalisation were sown a lot earlier than 1948, and go back to the very earliest days of the railways.

In the embryonic days of Britain's railway network, third-class passengers were carried in open trucks with benches fitted, as recreated at Didcot Railway Centre's broad gauge demonstration line, in this period train hauled by replica 2-2-2 *Fire Fly*. Gladstone's Railway Regulation Act of 1844 called for third-class passengers to be provided with protection from the weather, and seats. If the railway companies failed to comply, they ran the risk of being taken into state control. FRANK DUMBLETON/GWS

he produced a figure of £32,360 to build each mile, whereas in Belgium it had been done for £17,120. He also pointed out that fares in Belgium were roughly half of what they were in Britain.

The Act was passed in 1844 under Sir Robert Peel's Conservative government. Its primary purpose was to force the railways to reduce charges in the interests of the whole body of capitalist manufacturers and traders, by holding over their heads the threat of nationalisation.

It also enshrined in law the requirement to provide affordable ticket prices for the poorer sections of society, to enable them to travel to find work: before the coming of the railways, it was said that most people never ventured more than 15 miles beyond their place of birth.

Until that time there were three or more classes of carriage, third class was usually an open freight wagon.

Gladstone's Act, as it was also colloquially known, stipulated that one train with provision for carrying third-class passengers, should run on every line, every day, in each direction, stopping at every station, with a fare no more than a penny a mile and up to 56lb of luggage per passenger carried free of charge. The average speed should not be less than 12mph, and third-class passengers should be protected from the weather and be provided with seats.

In return, railway operators were exempted from duty on third-class passengers. These services became known as Parliamentary Trains. The Act's provision for nationalisation was never used, but it was there in the background as a threat, which could be used as a stick to beat the railway companies if they did not comply with other measures.

The reaction of many railway operators was grudging acceptance of the letter, if not the spirit of the legislation, and they provided the minimum one train per day with facilities for third-class passengers at an unpopular time such as early morning or late at night.

The companies were unhappy because they foresaw the prospect of losing revenue from ticket sales if passengers who could afford to travel second class switched to third, once facilities there became bearable. Indeed, certain companies continued to run inferior third- or fourth-class trains in addition to the minimum standard Parliamentary Train.

To place the liberating power of Gladstone's Act in a historical context, it was passed just two years after the Mines and Collieries Act of 1842.

In those formative years of the national railway network, never mind cheaper third-class travel tickets, the treatment of poorer members of the working class started at unthinkable on a good day, and went downhill from there. We often forget that back in the 1800s, the distinction between social classes was rigid and chasm-like, and there were many who feared that railways would bring the lower orders nearer to parity with their 'betters'.

At the dawn of the railway age, methods of coal extraction were primitive and the workforce of men, women and children, toiled in dangerous conditions. In 1841 around 216,000 people were employed in the mines. Women and children worked underground for 11 or 12 hours a day for lower wages than men.

It took an accident in 1838 to make the general public fully aware of conditions in the mines. At Huskar Colliery in Silkstone near Barnsley after a downpour from thunderstorms, a stream overflowed into the ventilation drift causing the death of 26 children; 11 girls aged from eight to 16, and 15 boys between nine and 12 years of age. Queen Victoria ordered an inquiry into the disaster.

Victorian society was shocked to discover that children, as young as five or six worked as trappers, opening and shutting ventilation doors down the mine before becoming hurriers, pushing and pulling coal tubs.

A Royal Commission headed by Lord Ashley published its report in 1842, and

The National Railway Museum's working replica of Stephenson's *Rocket* and two facsimile Liverpool & Manchester Railway coaches in action during a gala visit to the Great Central Railway in 2006. The success of the Liverpool & Manchester, the world's first inter-city line, sparked off the development of what would become Britain's national network. ROBIN JONES

A contemporary sketch shows the problem faced by a country where the railway network developed using two separate gauges. When Brunel's broad gauge met a standard gauge line, there could be no through running, and passengers and freight had to be taken off one train and placed on another.

rather than dwell on the safety aspects, in order to see legislation pushed through, he deliberately emphasised the affront to Victorian prudery, reporting on girls and woman wearing trousers and working bare-breasted in front of men and boys.

The 1842 Mines Act, which stemmed directly from his report, ruled that no children under the age of 10 were to be employed underground, but parish apprentices between the ages of 10 and 18 could continue to work in the mines.

Better travel for third-class passengers may be considered a trifling matter when compared with the appalling conditions that women and young children faced in the mines, but both were a step forward in the evolution of society.

Galt revised and republished his Railway Reform in 1864, and the following year, a Royal Commission was charged with looking again at nationalisation, only to conclude that no action was needed.

Journalist and businessman, Walter Bagehot, wrote in The Economist: "It is easy to show that the transfer of the railways to the state would be very beneficial, if only it can be effected."

It was in 1868 that the first nationalisation of any British industry took place, that of the telegraph network, which the government bought out from private companies. This nationalisation has been hailed as a precursor for the eventual taking of the railways into permanent state control.

THE GREAT RAILWAY FREE-FOR-ALL

At the time of Gladstone's Act, Britain's national network was still in its formative period, and comprised a growing portfolio of independent concerns made possible by free enterprise.

The opening of the world's first inter-city line, the Liverpool & Manchester Railway, was followed by the connecting Grand Junction Railway and London & Birmingham Railway, which formed the basis of today's West Coast Main Line, and many other trunk routes followed in their wake, often coming together – the East Coast Main Line a perfect example – on a piecemeal basis over many years.

While the government favoured the development of trunk railways to stimulate economic recovery and facilitate the movement of troops in times of potential civil unrest, it was legally required that each line be authorised by a separate Act of Parliament.

Although these Acts allowed railway companies powers of compulsory purchase, some powerful landowners objected to lines being built across their land and raised objections in Parliament to prevent Acts from being passed.

Some owners charged excessive amounts to sell the required strips of land, so these early lines did not always follow the optimal route. In addition,

steep gradients were to be avoided, as they would require more powerful and costlier locomotives with great coal consumption. Speeds were expected to be less than about 30mph, and in those early decades, curves were therefore considered less of a problem.

However, it was the sharp curves on these early lines that, a century later, would lead to British Railways' experimentation with tilting trains. If statutory powers to bulldoze through landowners' refusals to sell had been available then, such trains, like today's Virgin Pendolinos on the WCML, would never have been needed.

The boom years for railway growth were 1836 and 1845-47, the period of so-called Railway Mania, when Parliament authorised 8000 route miles at a projected cost of £200million, which was about the same value as the country's annual Gross Domestic Product (GDP) of the day.

While visionaries such as George and Robert Stephenson saw the day when a conglomeration of trunk routes would provide an inter-city network, it was shorter proposals that more easily attracted investors, whereby a clearly defined A-to-B line with an exact purpose promised swifter and more secure rewards.

Canal companies, unable or unwilling to upgrade their facilities to compete with railways, used political power to try to stop them. The railways responded by purchasing about a fourth

Brunel's broad gauge system was superior to others in many respects, yet it served only a fraction of the country. The last broad gauge 'Cornishman' is seen leaving Paddington at 10.15am on May 20, 1892, hauled by 4-2-2 *Great Western*. GWR

of the canal system, in part to get the right of way, and in part to pay off critics. By the 1840s, railway developers were in the driving seat, but without state regulation to prevent 'doubling up' of routes between major cities; they would become a major target for the Beeching Axe 120 years later.

Indeed, once an Act was obtained, there was little government regulation.

Neither was there, at the outset, a government policy about which gauge should be used: it was left to each individual railway to choose their own.

In the 1830s, when our railway network was starting to be built, there was no 'standard gauge', the term by which we refer George Stephenson's 4ft 8½in gauge today.

Great Western Railway engineer,

Isambard Kingdom Brunel, went his own way on many aspects of railway development, not least of all his use of rails that were 7ft 0¼in apart.

With locomotive wheels further apart, there would be more space to fit bigger and more powerful boilers between them. Furthermore, wheels mounted outside frames would cause less friction and lead to freer movement of trains.

Once the GWR main line from Paddington to Penzance had been converted from broad to standard gauge in May 1892, there was nowhere for the broad gauge rolling stock to run. Locomotives, carriages and wagons were all stored at Swindon Works to be scrapped. In its leader on May 23, 1892, The Times commented: "Uniformity of gauge is of the first importance in a country crossed and recrossed in every direction by networks of lines, which are of use to one another and to the public in just the degree in which they can be combined to form one harmonious whole." The question remains – might some form of state control early on have prevented the expansion of two disparate systems? GWR

Brunel's broad gauge network stretched from Paddington to Penzance in the west, Neyland in Pembrokeshire and Wolverhampton in the Midlands. However, while many engineers would have admired his system, railways serving the rest of Britain opted for standard gauge. That meant that there could be no through running between the Great Western system and the rest of the UK.

In 1845 a Gauge Commission was set up to report on whether all railways should be built to 'one uniform gauge'.

Brunel suggested that locomotive trials should be conducted to compare the merits of the two gauges.

The broad gauge tests were carried out between London and Didcot, and the locomotives proved able to pull heavier loads at higher speeds than their narrow gauge counterparts. Despite the outcome of these trials, the Gauge Commission declared that 4ft 8½in would become the standard, primarily because 87% of the nation's railways had already been built to that gauge.

I have always drawn parallels between the gauge issue and the home video recorder revolution of the late Seventies and Eighties. Experts would always tell you that the popular VHS offered the lesser quality of all the formats, while Betamax was far superior, while best of all was the little-used V5000 format. Yet the marketing of VHS won the day, leaving Betamax trailing in a poor second place and V5000 almost unheard of.

In the field of railways, standard gauge was cheaper to construct, and conversion from broad to narrow easier to carry out, as no additional trackbed widening would be required.

The GWR set about converting its lines at first to mixed gauge, by laying a third rail between the 7ft tracks, and then going the whole hog and adopting 4ft 8½in. The final route to be converted, the GWR main line from Paddington to Penzance, became standard gauge overnight on May 21-22, 1892, with the redundant broad gauge locomotives, carriages and wagons rendered fit for the scrapyard and were laid up in long sidings at Swindon Works waiting for the cutter's torch.

Had there been some form of state control over railway development, even if it had been limited to a rigid stipulation of what would be adopted as the 'national' gauge, who knows how the UK network might have turned out? As it was, the dawn of our railway network was in many aspects a free-for-all.

Chicken and egg time: history showed that the UK rail network evolved as an arbitrary affair, often to suit immediate local needs of the mid-19th century, and lacking in cohesion in its formative years. Yet in fairness, how could you nationalise a network which has yet to be?

The Midland Railway-Butterley's superb set of restored vintage Midland Railway wooden-bodied maroon coaches at Swanwick Junction. MIDLAND RAILWAY TRUST

TRANSPORT FOR THE PEOPLE

In a bold bid to lessen the Victorian class divides on board its trains, the Midland Railway went it alone, at first generating much resentment among its competitors. In its coaches it provided three compartments, glazed windows and an oil lamp in the roofs.

In 1875 the standard of third class was upgraded and second class was abolished, by relabelling the coaches.

The Midland's general manager, Sir James Allport, said: "If there is one part of my public life on which I look back with more satisfaction, it is with reference to the boon we conferred on third-class travellers..."

Other railways followed, albeit begrudgingly, and because they were obliged to provide third class, the oddity of first and third, but no second - except on boat trains - persisted into the 20th century, when third class was rebranded in 1956, and then further rebranded as 'standard' to remove negative associations. Social divides do not disappear overnight.

The Cheap Trains Act 1883 marked the beginning of workers' trains. It removed the passenger duty on any train charging less than a penny a mile and obliged the railway companies to operate a larger number of cheap trains, and in this respect went further than Gladstone's Act.

One major thrust of the 1883 Act was to tackle the problem of overcrowding in major cities, and local authorities sought to encourage working people to move to suburbia - even though many of them could not afford even a penny a mile to travel. Yet, the number of cheap suburban services increased, and helped promote the building of new housing estates on the green fringes of industrial cities, eventually paving the way for slum clearance.

During the 20th century, the appearance of competing road services meant that the railways were forced to reduce their fares, and so few services eventually attracted duty, that it was abolished in the Finance Act 1929.

The Midland Railway astonished and even angered its rivals by providing better coaches for third-class passengers in 1875. ROBIN JONES

THE FIRST STATE CONTROL... FOR THE TIME BEING

While railway owners and investors wanted to maximise their profits, the traders who had come to rely on them demanded lower charges, and regularly called on the government to exercise more control over railway pricings.

By Edwardian times, there were many who expressed the conviction that the British capitalists' problem of underselling the new great trading powers of Germany, the USA and Japan in the markets of the world could be made possible only by unification of inland transport under state ownership, or at second best close state control.

It was argued that national unification would eliminate wasteful competition and overlapping, and permit charges to be reduced. Liberal politicians and members of the then-new Labour Party backed up such calls from manufacturers and traders. However, state control was soon to become a reality, and not for reasons of commerce.

As the first decade of the 20th century passed, there were many who believed that Britain might be dragged into a European war, the like of which the world had never seen. Major powers would seek to use the technological fruits of the Industrial Revolution in terms of weaponry and transport to gain mastery over the continent and maybe beyond.

It went without saying that railways would play a major role in transporting troops, military equipment and horses both to the Channel embarkation ports, and around the country. Indeed, many of them had already been involved in the transport of many thousands of troops during annual manoeuvres.

In 1911, Britain's railway companies began to plan for potential mobilisation, and the mass movement of military trains to Southampton and other south coast ports. From experience gained through past movement of troops and equipment for military exercises, it was realised that better coordination and planning would be required if Britain was to enter into a future European war.

In 1912, the Railway Executive Committee was formed by the government to act as an intermediary between the War Office and the railway companies in order to oversee the planning and implementation of mobilisation. A master plan was drawn up, and orders were issued to the railway companies in what was known as the 'War Book'.

By that time, a series of alliances had gathered most of the world's technologically advanced countries into two potentially opposing power blocs, held together by a complicated series of alliances. It would take only a minor flashpoint to set them off against other, and that is exactly what happened.

On June 28, 1914, Archduke Franz Ferdinand, the heir to the throne of Austria-Hungary, was assassinated in the Bosnian capital, Sarajevo. The domino effect saw, within six weeks, the two power blocs at war.

The Allies, a bloc based on the United Kingdom of Britain and Ireland, the Triple Entente of the Russian Empire and the French Third Republic stood against the Central Powers of Germany and Austria-Hungary.

On August 4, 1914, war was declared –

Sir Herbert Ashcombe Walker, general manager of the London & South Western Railway, also served as acting chairman of the Railway Executive Committee.

and the same day, the Railway Executive Committee took control of the 130 companies that made up the national network for the first time.

Using powers enshrined in the Regulation of the Forces Act 1871, the committee could requisition any railway and its plant during a war, with provision for the payment of full compensation.

The application of these powers in August 1914 meant that, although the detailed management of the railways was left to the existing companies, the remuneration for the owners was fixed by the government, which could secure whatever priorities it required for different classes of traffic, a facility with economic as well as military significance.

The committee consisted of 11 of the general managers of the major railway companies. Locomotives, carriages and wagons, as well as workshops were given over to munitions work and locomotives were sent overseas for the war effort.

Railwaymen were encouraged to join the Royal Engineers, contributing to Army operations as part of the Railway Operating Division and delivering troops, ammunition and supplies to the front lines. Accordingly, many summer holiday services were suspended from August 4 and the winter timetable was implemented in many areas to save resources, as staff shortages quickly rose after an estimated 55,000 railwaymen joined up in the first few months.

At the start of the conflict, many volunteers joined the services supposedly safe in the knowledge that "it would all be over by Christmas".

If only.

The Westinghouse Brake Company reported that 118 or 28% of its staff had enlisted and that it was paying these men 50% of their wages and holding their jobs open for them until the end of the war. Altogether, during 1914-18, 184,475 or 49% of UK railway staff of military age enlisted.

Picked to chair the Railway Executive Committee was Sir Alexander Kaye Butterworth, LLB, OL (1854-1946) general manager of the North Eastern Railway.

Having qualified as a solicitor in 1883, and gained a law degree the following year, he joined the Great Western Railway's legal department. He moved to the NER as a solicitor in February 1891, where he was employed as a company solicitor at the inquiry into the railway accident at Thirsk the following year.

In 1905, he succeeded Sir George Gibb as general manager.

While chairman of the Railway Executive Committee until 1917, he also held his position at the NER, retiring from the company on December 31, 1921.

January 1917 saw Sir Herbert Ashcombe Walker (1868-1949), general manager of the London & South Western Railway since 1912, become acting chairman of the REC.

It was Walker who instigated the programme of third-rail electrification on parts of the LSWR.

In March 1915, he was knighted, and for his services to the REC, he was made a Knight Commander of the Order of the Bath (KCB).

Sir Eric Campbell Geddes in 1917.

UNDER ONE ROOF

Under the auspices of the Railway Executive Committee, from August 1914 millions of troops were moved by rail. The Great Eastern Railway, for example, operated 870 military trains in the first six weeks of the First World War, shifting 20,000 vehicles including wagons.

Winter timetables were introduced from September as this was a reduced service by comparison with the summer months.

The larger railway companies quickly built ambulance trains to carry wounded or sick members of the armed forces to and from ports. These steam-heated trains included a pharmacy, hot and cold water, electric lighting as well as day and night accommodation. They also had a kitchen and pantry car plus staff compartments. Carriages were equipped with sliding doors so stretchers could be used on and through the trains. These were often made from requisitioned parcels vans.

The wounded were returned to Southampton by ship where they were met by a dozen of these trains under the command of the surgeon general. He received lists of wounded twice a week as well as hospital bed availability and arranged suitable trains from Southampton around the UK to these hospitals.

The government relied on rail to send millions to the Western Front. At the start of the conflict, around 90 trains a day delivered tens of thousands of men to the docks at Southampton. On August 18 alone, 20,000 men, 1200 horses, 210 bicycles, 20 motorcars and 600 other vehicles passed through the port.

For the duration of the war, Britain fed around 2,500,000 men on the continent, with deliveries by rail. Overseen by former North Eastern

During the First World War, the need for a standard locomotive used in British military operations at home and overseas by the Railway Operating Division of the Royal Engineers was identified. Great Central Railway chairman, Sir Sam Fay, a member of the Railway Executive Committee, persuaded the government to choose his company's John G Robinson 8K 2-8-0 (LNER O4) for the purpose. Orders for 325 locomotives were placed in February 1917, and they were followed by orders for 196 more in 1918 in order to keep British industry going during the post-ar run-down in military manufacturing. After the war, the redundant 8Ks were loaned or sold to many of Britain's railways. As the price of war-surplus 8Ks plummeted, many ended up with the LNWR, its successor the LMS, the GWR and some were even sold as far afield as China and Australia, where three survive in preservation on static display. Here, the sole-surviving example in the UK, Robinson O4 No. 63601 storms towards Quorn & Woodhouse station during the Great Central Railway's 'Golden Oldies' gala on May 31, 2010. ROBIN JONES

No. 6311, which was built in 1919 to a government order, heads a train of empty mineral wagons at Worksop sidings on June 17, 1957. BEN BROOKSBANK*

A First World War ambulance train was recreated the National Railway Museum in York for a landmark exhibition, which opened on July 9, 2016, the centenary of the busiest day of the Battle of the Somme. The exhibition highlights the history and crucial role that ambulance trains played during the First World War and beyond. The carriage specially converted for the exhibition was once owned by the Ministry of Defence. Built in 1907 for the London & South Western Railway, it is of the type that would have been converted for use as an ambulance train. For the exhibition, it was carefully transformed both inside and out to enable visitors to step on board and move through a ward, a pharmacy and a nurses' mess room. Digital projection, sound and historic images, alongside recreated interior fittings recall the atmosphere of these confined trains. ROBIN JONES

Railway general manager, Sir Eric Campbell Geddes (1875-1937), as Inspector General of the British Expeditionary Force, a network was established to transport millions upon millions of shells to the trenches to supply the endless artillery bombardments.

Under Geddes, thousands of miles of narrow-gauge railways were laid to enable greater flexibility of supply trains coming up to the Western Front. Armoured petrol-powered locomotives were developed in place of steam to avoid the enemy guns on the trench lines.

Geddes served as British minister of munitions, inspector general of transportation, Controller of the Navy and finally First Lord of the Admiralty during the war.

His career with the NER had begun in 1904, and 10 years later, he had graduated to the company's top job.

David Lloyd George, the minister of munitions who was always on the lookout for "men of push and go" brought in Geddes to serve in his department as deputy director of supply, before being dispatched to France in 1916 as Inspector General of Sir Douglas Haig's British Expeditionary Force. For this role he was awarded the honorary title Major-General.

As Inspector-General, Geddes revolutionised the BEF's transport and supply mechanism, dividing transportation into four separate areas to cover docks, light railways, railways and roads, while employing his favoured methods of statistical analysis. By the time he left this role in 1917 (the same year his younger brother, Sir Auckland Geddes, was appointed minister of National Service) efficiency had been transformed.

Geddes left the Admiralty in early 1918 but retained his post in Lloyd George's Imperial War Cabinet until the end of the war. He gained fame for his publicly stated promise of "squeezing" Germany "until the pips squeak".

As the conflict worsened, ambulance trains were sent to France to bring home the more seriously wounded using cross-Channel train ferries. Again, here was another sector in which wartime traffic boomed.

A new port was built at Richborough in Kent to handle train ferry services.

Thousands of British railwaymen operated the railways in France using UK locomotives exported by the Army. In all, the military took more than 600 locomotives.

Under the committee, the Grand Fleet based on Scapa Flow was supplied with coal by 'Jellicoe specials', mostly from the GWR's Pontypool Road depot in South Wales to Grangemouth, on the Caledonian Railway, a distance of 375 miles.

From August 1914 to March 1919, 13,630 coal specials were run from South Wales to Scotland using West Coast, East Coast, and Midland routes. Large quantities of equipment, including shells and fuses, were manufactured in railway works.

A particular problem was presented by large volumes of passenger and

Protected Motor-Rail petrol tractor No. 1381 of 1918 No. LR3101 visiting the 2014 Tracks to the Trenches gala at the Apedale Valley Light Railway near Stoke-on-Trent from the Amberley Museum & Heritage Centre in Sussex. Built for the Western Front, it did not get any further to the action than Purfleet Wharf in Essex. However, it was typical of the internal combustion locomotives employed in the trench railways of the First World War. Unlike steam locomotives, they did not give their location away to the enemy. ROBIN JONES

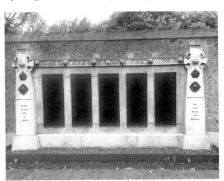

The memorial to the victims of the Quintinshill rail disaster at Rosebank cemetery in Edinburgh, where they were buried near their home town of Leith. ROBIN JONES

A Great Western Railway ambulance train, as depicted in a hand-coloured postcard. Such trains were run by all the major British railway companies to take wounded soldiers back to their home towns. ROBIN JONES COLLECTION

freight traffic arising at ordnance factories that had been set up at places with few existing railway facilities, as in the Gretna area.

The First World War also saw the worst rail disaster in British history. A five-train crash at Quintinshill near Gretna Green in Dumfriesshire on May 22, 1915 caused 226 deaths and left 246 injured. The majority of the fatalities were soldiers from the Royal Scots regiment, who had been travelling on one of the two trains involved in the first collision.

The initial investigation laid the blame for the accident with two signalmen, George Meakin and James Tinsley, who were later prosecuted and imprisoned for criminal negligence. Railway safety improvements such as the use of track circuits and signaller reminder devices were introduced to prevent similar railway accidents in the future.

Overall, however, the centralised control of the UK rail network during the war had been so successful that there were those who called for the arrangement to be made permanent.

The state control of the railways, which began under war conditions were, under the Ministry of Transport Act 1919, to continue for a further two years.

The wreckage of a locomotive dominates the horizon after the collision at Quintinshill on May 22, 1915, Britain's worst-ever rail disaster. ILLUSTRATED LONDON NEWS

An aerial view of the GWR's Swindon Works in the 1920s. Brunel's great workshop found itself at the heart of a much wider railway empire following the Grouping of 1923.

THE GROUPING

David Lloyd George, prime minister of the wartime coalition government from 1916-22, was sympathetic to trade union calls for nationalisation of the railway network.

In December 1916, the Liberal David Lloyd George formed a coalition government and was appointed prime minister by King George V.

His administration replaced the earlier wartime coalition under Herbert Asquith, which had been held responsible for losses during the war.

At the end of the conflict, not only the railways but the coal mines were under state control. Railwaymen and miners were campaigning for permanent nationalisation.

In March 1918, Lloyd George told a Trade Union Congress deputation on nationalisation of railways and canals that, "he was in complete sympathy with the general character of the proposals put forward."

During the 1918 general election, at Dundee on December 4, Winston Churchill – then still a Liberal minister stated – "that the Government policy was the nationalisation of the railways."

Several other ministers also called for the railways to be nationalised.

The Ways and Communications Bill of February 1919 went as far as to include powers of state purchase, but it was not to be.

In July 1919 Andrew Bonar Law, leader of the Conservative Party, declared his opposition to railway nationalisation. Churchill's protests were in vain, and the power to nationalise was dropped from the bill.

As we have seen, state control of the network through the REC remained in place until 1921. It was in that year that a 'compromise solution' or half-way house to nationalisation was chosen.

The government introduced the Railways Act 1921, which compelled the 120 railway companies then operating to merge into just four.

The wording of the Act had been developed by Geddes, in his role as minister of transport.

Minister of Munitions Winston Churchill meets female workers at Georgetown's filling works near Glasgow during a visit on October 9, 1918. As a Liberal minister, he stated that government policy was nationalising the railways.

Andrew Bonar Law, Conservative prime minister from October 23, 1922 to May 22, 1923, opposed the nationalisation of railways.

In contrast to the concept of all-out nationalisation, Geddes favoured privately owned regional monopolies through amalgamations, and suggested increased worker participation from prewar levels.

Yes, he viewed the prewar competition between the many individual railway companies as wasteful, but was opposed to nationalisation on the grounds that it led to poor management, as well as a corrupting influence between railway and political interests.

In his cabinet paper, Future Transport Policy, published on March 9, 1920, Geddes had proposed five English groups (Southern, Western, North Western, Eastern and North Eastern), a London passenger group, and separate single groupings for Scotland and Ireland.

These proposals became the 1920 white paper, Outline of Proposals as to the Future Organisation of Transport Undertakings in Great Britain and their Relation to the State. The paper suggested the formation of six or seven regional companies, plus worker participation on the board of directors of the company.

However, the white paper was opposed by the Railway Companies' Association and MPs representing railway operators' interests.

The move to greater worker participation was particularly opposed by the RCA, but supported by the Labour party. Worker-directors were not included in the final act, being replaced by agreed negotiating mechanisms.

The regional groups initially proposed in the white paper were five in England (Southern, Western, North-western, Eastern, and North-eastern), and a Scottish regional group.

Railways serving London were intended to form a separate regional group, but this amalgamation was delayed and took place under the

London Passenger Transport Act 1933.

In 1921, a subsequent white paper, Memorandum on Railways Bill, suggested four English regional groups and two Scottish groups. However, Scottish railway companies wished to be incorporated into British groupings, and it was eventually decided that they would be included with the Midland/North western and Eastern groups, so that the three main Anglo-Scottish trunk routes, the West and East Coast main lines and the Midland Main Line, should each be owned by one company for its full length.

The first paragraph of the Railways Act of 1921 states: "With a view to the reorganisation and more efficient and economical working of the railway system of Great Britain railways shall be formed into groups in accordance with the provisions of this Act, and the principal railway companies in each group shall be amalgamated, and other companies absorbed in a manner provided by this Act."

The third reading of the Act in the Commons took place on August 9, 1921, and was passed with a majority of 237 to 62. It was then passed to the House of Lords where amendments were made, and these were accepted by the Commons on August 19 and Royal Assent given.

The Act came into effect on January 1, 1923. On that date most of the mergers between the individual companies took place, although some had occured during the previous year. The four 'super companies' comprised the Great Western and Southern railways, and two wholly new companies, the London, Midland and Scottish and the London & North Eastern railways.

The February 1923 issue of The Railway Magazine dubbed the new joint stock public companies as "The Big Four of the New Railway Era", and the term Big Four is still used today to describe them.

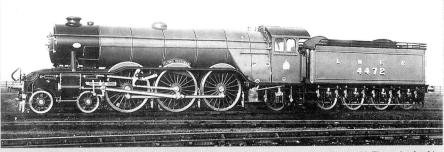

A locomotive that spanned the 1923 Grouping ended up being the most famous in the world. The order for A1 Pacific Flying Scotsman was placed by the Great Northern Railway in 1922, but the locomotive was completed in the early days of the LNER. At first it carried the GNR number 1472, because the LNER had not yet decided on a system-wide numbering scheme. In February 1924 it was allocated the LNER number 4472 and named after one of the company's famous trains. As such it quickly became a flagship locomotive for the LNER. As pictured here, it represented the company at the British Empire Exhibition at Wembley Park in 1924 and 1925, and was regularly used for promotional purposes, years before it became the first locomotive in the world to officially reach 100mph, on November 30, 1934. However, Flying Scotsman had already acquired legendary status. It hauled the inaugural non-stop 'Flying Scotsman' over the 392 miles from King's Cross to Edinburgh Waverley on May 1, 1928, in eight hours. Its designer, Nigel Gresley, was Chief Mechanical Engineer of both the GNR and LNER. At the Grouping, the post at the LNER had originally been offered to the elderly John G Robinson, who turned it down and suggested the much-younger Gresley.

EXEMPTIONS TO THE GROUPING

Several lines that had been jointly owned by pre-Grouping companies did not become part of the Big four, but continued to be run as partnerships by successor companies.

These were the Midland & Great Northern Joint Railway, run jointly by the LMS and LNER, the Cheshire Lines Committee, the Somerset & Dorset Joint Railway, run jointly by the Southern Railway and LMS, Great Western & Great Central Joint Railway, which was run by the GWR and LNER, and the Manchester, South Junction & Altrincham Railway, which passed to the control of the LNER and LMS.

London's suburban railway companies, such as the Underground Electric Railways Company and the Metropolitan Railway, were also excluded from the 1921 Act, but under the London Passenger Transport Act 1933 were amalgamated along with the capital's bus and tram operations into the London Passenger Transport Board.

Two other electric railways were left out: the Liverpool Overhead Railway and the Mersey Railway.

Derby-built Somerset & Dorset Joint Railway 4-4-0 No. 77 of 1908, carrying the company's trademark Prussian blue livery. The Somerset & Dorset was among those lines that continued to be run jointly after the Grouping. No. 77 acquired the LMS number 320 and was withdrawn in the Thirties. ROBIN JONES COLLECTION

Light railways, which had been authorised under the 1896 Light Railways Act, were also left out of the 1921 Act.

These lines were built "on the cheap" to serve towns and rural areas that the larger railway companies did not consider economically worthy of their attention. The 1896 Act was passed a few years before the emergence of motor road transport, which especially in the years after the First World War, became a serious competitor to all railways, with the market being flooded with secondhand military transport lorries.

It was the legendary light railway empire builder, Col Holman F Stephens, who played a major part in getting exemption for them. However, many light railways succumbed to the far more versatile road transport and closed in the Twenties and Thirties because they could not pay.

During the war, many classes of locomotives were painted in plain black, to save money on maintenance. No exception was made for the glamorous streamliners from the golden age of steam in the Thirties. Outshopped from Crewe on June 26, 1943, the year in which the works celebrated its centenary, LMS Princess Coronation Pacific No. 6245 *City of London* was the first streamliner to be painted in wartime unlined black, with lettering and number in red-shaded yellow. The wartime black livery also marked the passing of an era in which railways such as the LNER and LMS placed a high PR value on the appearance of prestigious express passenger locomotives. Rivalries on routes such as the East and West Coast main lines had gone, never to return. In its rebuilt form, in 1957, *City of London* became the first Duchess to be painted in British Railways' maroon, but with LMS-style lining and never the BR pattern. Withdrawn on September 12, 1964, ironically it was one of the last three Duchesses to be based in London. THE RAILWAY MAGAZINE

CONSTITUENT COMPANIES OF THE BIG FOUR

GREAT WESTERN RAILWAY

Great Western Railway	3005 miles
Alexandra Docks & Railway	10.5 miles
Barry Railway	68 miles
Cambrian Railways	295.25 miles
Cardiff Railway	11.75 miles
Rhymney Railway	51 miles
Taff Vale Railway	124.5 miles

LONDON & NORTH EASTERN RAILWAY

Great Central Railway	852.5 miles
Great Eastern Railway	1191.25 miles
Great Northern Railway	1051.25 miles
Hull & Barnsley Railway	106.5 miles
North Eastern Railway	1757.75 miles
Great North of Scotland Railway	334.5 miles
North British Railway	1378 miles

LONDON, MIDLAND & SCOTTISH RAILWAY

London & North Western Railway (including Lancashire and Yorkshire Railway amalgamated from January 1, 1922)	2667.5 miles
Furness Railway	158 miles
Midland Railway	2170.75 miles
North Staffordshire Railway	220.75 miles
Caledonian Railway	1114.5 miles
Glasgow and South Western Railway	493.5 miles
Highland Railway	506 miles

IRISH LINES ABSORBED BY THE LMS WERE:

Dundalk, Newry and Greenore Railway	26.5 miles
Northern Counties Committee lines	265.25 miles
Joint Midland & Great Northern Railway (Ireland) lines	

SOUTHERN RAILWAY

London, Brighton & South Coast Railway	457.25 miles
London & South Western Railway	1020.5 miles
South Eastern & Chatham Railway (a working union of the South Eastern Railway and the London, Chatham & Dover Railway)	637.75 miles

LIGHT RAILWAYS EXCLUDED FROM THE GROUPING

STANDARD GAUGE

Bideford, Westward Ho! & Appledore Railway (closed at time of Grouping)	7 miles
Bishops Castle Railway	9.75 miles
Corringham Light Railway	2.75 miles
Derwent Valley Light Railway	16 miles
Easingwold Railway	2.5 miles
East Kent Railway	48 miles
Glasgow (Cable) Subway	6.75 miles
Hellingly Hospital Railway	1.25 miles
Hundred of Manhood & Selsey Tramways	8 miles
Kent & East Sussex Railway	24 miles
Mumbles Railway	5.5 miles
Nidd Valley Light Railway	
North Sunderland Railway	
Rowrah & Kelton Fell Railway	
Shropshire & Montgomeryshire Railway	26 miles
Stocksbridge Railway	2 miles
Swansea Improvements & Tramways Company	18 miles
Wantage Tramway	2 miles
Weston, Clevedon & Portishead Railway	14.5 miles

NARROW GAUGE

Ashover Light Railway, 2ft	7.25 miles
Brighton (Volks) Electric Railway, 2ft 8.5in	1.75 miles
Camborne & Redruth Tramway, 3ft 6in	3.25 miles
Campbeltown & Machrihanish Railway, 2ft 3in	6 miles
Corris Railway, 2ft 3in	11 miles
Ravenglass & Eskdale Railway, 15in	7.25 miles
Ffestiniog Railway, 1ft 11½	14.5 miles
Glyn Valley Tramway, 2ft 4.5in	8.25 miles
North Wales Narrow Gauge Railways, 1ft 11½in	12.25 miles
Portmadoc, Beddgelert & South Snowdon Railway, 1ft 11½in	4.75 miles
Rye & Camber Tramway, 3ft	3 miles
Snailbeach District Railways, 2ft 4in	3.25 miles
Snowdon Mountain Railway, 2ft 7½ in	5 miles
Southwold Railway, 3ft	9 miles
Talyllyn Railway, 2ft 3in	
Wolverton and Stony Stratford Tramway, 3ft 6in (owned by LMS).	

OTHER PRIVATE RAILWAYS

Felixstowe Docks & Railway	0.5 mile
Manchester Ship Canal Railway	156 miles
Mersey Docks & Harbour Board	104 miles
Milford Haven Dock & Railway	1.25 miles
Pentewan Railway (2ft 6 in gauge)	
Trafford Park	18 miles

RAILWAYS OUTSIDE THE JURISDICTION OF UK PARLIAMENT

Alderney Railway	2 miles
Guernsey Railway	3 miles
Isle of Man Railway (3ft gauge)	46.25 miles
Jersey Eastern Railway	6.25 miles
Jersey Railway & Tramways, 3ft 6in	7.5 miles
Manx Electric Railway 3ft	18 miles
and 3ft 6in	5 miles

The Weston, Clevedon & Portishead Railway was one of several light railways that remained unaffected by the Grouping. It was likely that they were considered loss-making concerns of little strategic or economic value apart from services to very local communities. This line opened in 1897 and lived a hand-to-mouth existence. Even light railway empire builder Col Holman F Stephens could not make it pay and it closed in 1940. It was taken over by the GWR, which used it purely for wagon storage, and the track was lifted for use in the war effort between October 1942 and late 1943. Despite its lossmaking nature, this very rural railway provided the only direct link between the three coastal towns. In that respect it has never been replaced. Pictured is secondhand 1876-built Sharp Stewart 0-4-2ST *Hesperus*, which worked on the line between 1931-37.
PAUL TOWNSEND*

SECOND WORLD WAR

The Railway Executive Committee may have ceased to run Britain's railways in 1921, but it had not gone away, and was to return again in Britain's darkest hour.

In the years that followed Hitler's rearmament of Germany, those in the UK's corridors of power who feared that a second world war was inevitable steadily grew in numbers.

The Big Four saw the darkening clouds on the eastern horizon and had been preparing for a fresh conflict for some years.

Comprehensive evacuation plans had been prepared well before September 1939 so when war broke out on the third of that month, the railways already knew full well what was expected of them.

The REC had been reformed on September 24, 1938 with a new remit to run the network if war broke out. The railways would later be brought under government control through the REC under the direction of the Ministry of Transport.

Initially the role of the REC this time round was advisory, centring on the coordination of existing emergency plans and preparations of the railway companies and the Railway Technical Committee for civilian evacuation and air raid precautions.

Minister of Transport Euan Wallace took control of the railways on September 1, 1939, two days before Britain declared war on Germany. Control was taken using the Emergency (Railway Control) Order under the powers granted by the Emergency Powers (Defence) Act 1939.

The Big Four were immediately placed under central government command with representatives of each major railway taking a place at the General Manager's Conference, as it was known.The Big Four were initially represented by Sir Ralph Wedgwood (chairman) for the LNER, Sir James Milne (deputy chairman) for the GWR, Sir William Wood for the LMS, Gilbert Szlumper for the SR, and Frank Pick for the London Passenger Transport Board. G Cole Deacon from the Railway Companies Association was the committee's secretary.

In addition to the Big Four other railways that were considered to be of strategic importance were also taken into government control. They were the East Kent Railway, the Kent & East Sussex Railway, the King's Lynn Docks and Railway Company, the Mersey Railway and the Shropshire and Montgomery Railway.

All railway assets had been turned over to the war effort by the start of 1940 with many railwaymen joining up and their shipping fleets often

BELOW: On April 20, 1941, GWR 4-6-0 No. 4911 *Bowden Hall* took a direct hit during a bombing raid on the Keyham area of Plymouth and was later broken up. The locomotive had stopped at a signalbox because of an air raid, and the crew survived by sheltering under the steps of the signalbox. At the same time, sister No. 4936 *Kinlet Hall*, accidentally ran into a bomb crater in that area and was severely damaged, but was repaired into service and survives in preservation today.
MAURICE DART/COLOUR RAIL

Forces personnel waiting for trains were an everyday sight in wartime. Here, 1905-built Ivatt C1 4-4-2 No. 4411 pulls into Royston station in 1944. Nine years before, on June 15, 1935, No. 4411 was hauling a passenger train that was hit by an express passenger train at Welwyn Garden City after a signalman's error. Fourteen people were killed and 29 were injured. This locomotive survived the Second World War by only two years, being withdrawn from King's Cross shed on August 31, 1947.
COLOUR RAIL

commandeered for military purposes. As in the First World War, the many railway works became huge military factories. A total of 642 tanks were built at Crewe and Horwich, while Swindon and Doncaster turned out guns and gun mountings. Shells, bridges, ball bearings and landing craft were built at Eastleigh and Swindon.

At Ebbw Junction, the US Army Transportation Corps used railway workshops for assembling its equipment.

Yet the Second World War was to be a markedly different conflict as compared with 1914-18. This time round, aerial bombardment was to be a major threat, and so the use of lights in railway operations after dark had to be restricted, thereby creating dangerous working conditions for staff.

Many freight services were switched to running in daytime because of the blackout restrictions and experiments were made with blue bulbs and emergency lighting installed in carriages. Master switches were

installed in carriages so if an air raid warning was given, one switch could plunge a train into darkness.

Station lamps had shades fitted to stop their light going upwards. On locomotives, light sheets were placed between the cab roof and the tender, hiding the glow from the firebox, creating appalling working conditions.

Around 10% of railway staff were given air raid precautions training and toured the network with specially equipped instruction trains. The railway telephone system was integrated with the Post Office to ensure continuity after bomb damage.

Strategic materials were stockpiled at key locations around the network so that any damage could be repaired quickly and efficiently.

Emergency repair trains and cranes were deployed around the network for the same reason.

Southampton Docks had been modernised a few years earlier and was the largest in the world and

very strategically placed. Rail links to the port were to be of paramount importance.

Removal of the contents of factories, farms (complete with their livestock) and households comprised a major part of the network's freight, notwithstanding the needs of the military.

Preparing for war, the railways had recently built many high-capacity wagons, the largest of which had 56 wheels and could carry 150 tons.

At stations, hundreds of thousands of military personnel were fed at special prices as refreshment rooms stayed open for longer hours.

In the first four months of the war, 8000 special troop trains operated and railway communications were linked directly with the War Office. The railways played a major role in the evacuation of more than 300,000 soldiers from Dunkirk between May 27 and June 4, 1940.

After the fall of France in June 1940, the invasion of Britain seemed

ABOVE: When the National Railway Museum publicly unveiled *Flying Scotsman* on May 27, 2011, following a major overhaul, it appeared in wartime black livery as No. 103, and was to have run on the national network as such for a period of time. However, within weeks of this high-profile relaunch, a series of major faults were found with the locomotive and a fresh overhaul had to start, delaying its comeback until early 2016. ROBIN JONES

LEFT: World steam railway speed record-holder *Mallard* was cosmetically restored for the 2013 Great Gathering of all six LNER A4 streamlined Pacifics, including the two 'exiled' in North American museums, to mark the 75th anniversary of *Mallard*'s historic 126mph run. The then National Railway Museum director, Steve Davies, who had set up the hugely successful event, took the opportunity to parade No. 4468 in black undercoat, very similar to the wartime black livery carried by all members of the class during the Second World War to reduce maintenance costs, while it was being repainted blue for the big occasion. ROBIN JONES

A Dornier Do 217 picked its way through barrage balloons and dropped a stick of bombs on to Middlesbrough station 1940.

BELOW: Sir Winston Churchill entertained future US president Dwight D. Eisenhower, then the Supreme Commander of the Allied Forces in Europe, in 1940-built GWR Special Saloon No. W9001 during the Second World War. Now preserved at the Buckinghamshire Railway Centre in pristine condition following restoration, the coach still has its lounge, dining room, kitchen and pantry.
ANDREW BRATTON

more likely than not. Twelve armoured trains carrying anti-aircraft guns were deployed on the east and south-east coasts and in Scotland and even the 15in gauge Romney Hythe & Dymchurch Railway was pressed into military service because of its strategic position on an exposed Kent coast.

This time round, more men were exempted from conscription because they were in reserved occupations. Nevertheless, the Big Four released around 110,000 staff for National Service, with 100,000 of them going into the forces, as well as providing 298 steam and 45 diesel locomotives for service overseas.

MIDDLESBROUGH BOMB

Middlesbrough was the first major British town and industrial target to be bombed during the Second World War. The Luftwaffe first attacked it on May 25, 1940 when a lone bomber dropped

13 bombs between South Bank Road and the South Steel Plant. The bomber was forced to leave after RAF night fighters were scrambled to intercept.

On January 15, 1942, minutes after being hit by gunfire from a merchant ship anchored off Hartlepool, a Dornier Do 217 collided with the cable of a barrage balloon over the River Tees. The blazing bomber plummeted on to the railway sidings in South Bank leaving a crater 12ft deep. In 1997 the remains of the Dornier were unearthed by a group of workers clearing land for redevelopment.

On August 4 that same year another Dornier Do 217 picked its way through barrage balloons and dropped a stick of bombs on to the town's station. One bomb caused serious damage to the Victorian glass and steel roof. A train in the station was also badly damaged although there were no passengers on board.

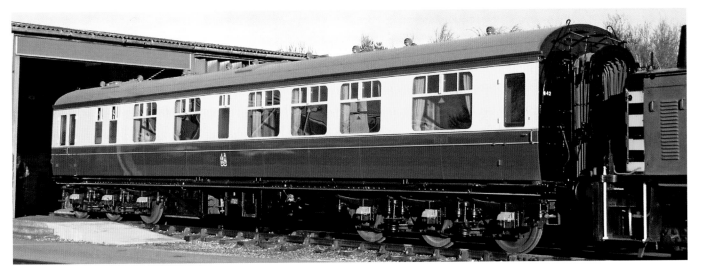

STANIER 8F 2-8-0

The LMS Stanier 8F 2-8-0 was to the Second World War what the Great Central Robinson 8K 2-8-0 was to the First World War.

It was a phenomenally successful heavy-freight version of William Stanier's go-anywhere, do-anything LMS 'Black Five' 4-6-0s, which were largely based on the GWR Hall class. They first appeared in 1934 and the last of 852 in 1951.

The War Department chose the Stanier 8F as Britain's standard freight design at the start of the Second World War, and requisitioned 51 Crewe and Vulcan Foundry-built examples and ordered 208 from Beyer Peacock and the North British Locomotive Company,

Production of 8Fs for the War Department continued until 1943, when the first of Robert Riddles' cheaper WD Austerity 2-8-0s appeared.

The Railway Executive Committee ordered Stanier 8Fs to be built at the works of all of the Big Four companies rather than just the LMS. Having unified control of the country's railways allowed the REC to be able to do so.

The GWR's Swindon Works turned out 80, as did the LNER's Darlington Works. The LNER's Doncaster Works produced 30, while the Southern Railway built 23 at Eastleigh, 14 at Ashford and 68 at Brighton, all on REC orders. For the LNER, which classified them O6, Brighton Works built 25, the company's own Darlington Works 23 and Doncaster another 20.

The War Department originally ordered Stanier 8Fs for service in support of the British Expeditionary Force, but they were not ready until after Dunkirk and the surrender of France. They were, however, shipped to Egypt, Palestine, Iran and Italy for military purposes, mostly as kits of parts to be assembled when they reached their destinations, and after the war, many were sold to these countries' railways. Turkey and Iraq also bought examples.

Eventually, the Middle East Forces' 8F fleet totalled 90. After the war ended, 39 were sold in 1948 to the new British Railways, and five were brought home in 1952 for War Department use. They were in poor condition, and were refurbished for WD use at the Longmoor Military Railway in Hampshire.

Three of these were sold to British Railways in 1957 and became Nos. 48773-75. The other two were transferred to the Cairnryan Military Railway and were scrapped in 1959, and so the War Department's use of Stanier 8Fs came to an end, 14 years after the end of the war.

Stanier 8F No. 48431 (pictured) is the only surviving Second World War Swindon-built example. Dating from 1944, it is displayed in the Keighley & Worth Valley Railway's exhibition shed at Oxenhope station. ROBIN JONES

LMS Stanier 8F No. 48773 is displayed inside the Severn Valley Railway's Engine House museum and visitor centre at Highley opposite War Department Austerity 2-10-0 No. WD600 Gordon, which also worked on the Longmoor Military Railway. In October 2011, the 1940-built 8F, which was ordered from the North British Locomotive Company of Glasgow by the War Department, became the focal point of a service in the Engine House honouring nine people who died during the Battle of Britain when a Luftwaffe bomber attacked the Melbourne Military Railway near Castle Donington in Derbyshire. SVR

GOING UNDERGROUND

At first, the offices of the revived Railway Executive Committee were at Fielden House in Great College Street, Westminster.

Unlike the railway companies, which were planning to move their headquarters out of London, a prime Luftwaffe target, the REC remained in London to stay in close contact with the government.

The basement in Fielden House was unsuitable, so the disused Down Street tube station was converted into bomb-proof underground offices to become the REC headquarters.

Down Street station was opened in 1907 by the Great Northern, Piccadilly & Brompton Railway, and was in its final years served by the Piccadilly line. However, patronage was poor, so much so that it was often missed out by passing trains.

The station closed as early as May 21, 1932, but its finest hour by far was yet to come.

The station was selected for use as a bomb-proof underground bunker in early 1939, as part of a programme of developing deep shelters to protect government operations from bombing in the event of war.

In the mid-Thirties, Winston Churchill often found himself a lone voice at Westminster, warning about the rise of Nazi Germany, yet as time passed, others began to publicly share his concerns, to the point where the Chamberlain government – far from

unanimously believing in "peace in our time" – began to prepare for the day when war would break out again.

Sir Ralph Wedgwood suggested that the REC should also relocate to safer accommodation, maybe Guildford or Rickmansworth, to protect its telephone exchange, which would be crucial if the country came under attack.

The basement in Fielden House, the first option to be considered in depth, was unsuitable – Scotland Yard warned of the flooding risk and the building's vulnerability to aerial attack - so disused Down Street was selected for

conversion into underground offices to house the REC headquarters. A lease with London Transport was signed on March 28, 1939, and the LMS drew up a blueprint for its conversion.

The only available space was on the platforms, but Piccadilly Line trains still passed through the station. With great secrecy, new walls were built at night when the trains had stopped running.

The doors to the new headquarters were fitted with gas locks, air filtration and short, secret, platforms were added, from which REC members and senior staff could stop a train and travel in

This tunnel at Down Street tube station was converted into a room where Winston Churchill would spend the night. He was here on November 19, 1940, a particularly bad night of the Blitz. ROBIN JONES

The forerunner to British Railways. This view, taken in the committee room at the Railway Executive Committee's Down Street station headquarters on April 26, 1940, shows (left to right): Sir Eustace J Missenden, (SR); Sir James Milne, (GWR deputy chairman); Sir William Wood, (LMSR); Mr W H Mills, (REC minute clerk); E G Marsden, (REC assistant to secretary); Sir Charles H Newton, (LNER); Frank Pick, (London Transport); Sir Ralph Wedgwood, LNER general manager (and first REC chairman); G Cole Deacon, (REC secretary); and VM Barrington Ward (chairman of the Operating Committee). Decisions affecting the nation's railway network during the Second World War were being made from a tube station that had closed seven years before hostilities broke out. LONDON TRANSPORT MUSEUM

the cab to the next station. The new headquarters included meeting rooms and offices, dormitories, dining facilities, kitchens, and mess rooms.

The site was equipped with its own telephone exchange connected to 50 telephones and a teletype machine, so it could send missives to the railway network. The postal address of Down Street was kept secret, so

Chris Nix, London Transport Museum's assistant director of collections and engagement, shows guests the interior of the bomb-proof rooms deep underground in Down Street station where Churchill and the Railway Executive Committee made key decisions for the national rail network that could impact on the future of the war, as bombs were dropping on London above. ROBIN JONES

post was taken to and from site by a dedicated team of four London Tran sport motorcycle dispatch riders who carried letters on a circuit between stations, head offices and government buildings.

The rooms were kitted out to a high standard by LMS carriage fitters who plastered, painted or panelled over most of the original tiled walls. Main offices

and mess rooms were fitted with radio sets connected to a receiving aerial above ground.

REC staff worked shifts to provide continuous 24/7 operation and to avoid attracting attention by the sight of a constant stream of people entering a disused station, most staff were also required to live and sleep there. A total of 19 staff dormitory rooms were provided, eight of which accommodated three people in shared, tiered bunk beds.

Only the executive members of staff had bedrooms to themselves.

Catering was provided by a kitchen at platform level, serving a staff mess room and an executive mess room. Food came via the railway hotels and was of a good standard.

During the Blitz, which lasted from September 1940 to March 1941, the amount of high-explosive, incendiary bombs and parachute mines falling on Whitehall damaged 10 Downing Street to the point that Churchill had to move out while the building was repaired and strengthened.

While work was underway to strengthen the Cabinet War Rooms, they would not have been able to survive a direct hit from a large bomb.

In mid-October 1940, Sir Ralph's brother Josiah Wedgwood, persuaded Churchill that the REC headquarters

The front of Down Street station as it appeared in July 1907, four months after it opened on March 17 that year. Little did passers-by in the early Forties realise that crucial decisions about the future of their country and the war against Nazi Germany were being made inside. LONDON TRANSPORT MUSEUM

The front of long-closed Down Street station today. The modern-day entrance to the old tube station that became Churchill's bunker is on the left of the Mayfair mini shop. ROBIN JONES

at Down Street would make the ideal shelter for him.

So, between October and December 1940, Churchill used Cole Deacon's office at Down Street as his sleeping quarters. On November 19 that year, the prime minster dined there with members of the REC and the War Cabinet who were served caviar, Perrier Jouet 1928 champagne, 1865 brandy and fine cigars.

Churchill called Down Street "The Barn", but he was so impressed by the REC's Down Street headquarters during the many nights he spent in it, that he asked for special quarters for his own use to be provided there.

Despite reservations by London Transport engineers, that using the only spare passageway left free would cause problems with the use of the station for the ventilation of the Piccadilly Line, the work was approved on January 22, 1941, and was completed ahead of its six-week schedule.

It was all in vain, however, for by the time Churchill's personal quarters had been completed, reinforcement of the Cabinet War Rooms had finished, and the prime minster therefore had no further need for Down Street.

Nonetheless, the REC was able to carry out its vital duties throughout the war from Down Street, not bothered by air raids. From there, it administered the movement of ambulance trains, food trains, munitions and personnel.

It also had to ensure the smooth running of the operation of the network in wartime, such as arranging for milk supplies to be rerouted, so that it was not wasted when a railway line had been bombed, or whether directional notices telling passengers to keep to the left should include 'keep left' notices in French and Polish.

No bombs ever fell directly on Down Street, and so the effectiveness of its reinforced shielding was never tested.

The operation from the disused tube station was so successful that the REC stayed there after the war was over, not leaving until New Year's Eve 1947.

After that, unwanted and unloved Down Street station went back to its main prewar use as a giant ventilation shaft for the Piccadilly Line. Today, it is regularly opened for guided tours run by London Transport Museum.

A DEFEAT IN VICTORY

Between the two world wars, the financial position of Britain's railways had deteriorated. Under the control of the Railway Executive Committee during the Second World War, the railways carried an extremely heavy burden with a remarkable degree of confidence and a good safety record. In 1944, for example 50% more freight was carried than in 1938.

The austerity of the war years took its toll though, and by the end of hostilities in 1945, much of the network's infrastructure and rolling stock was looking worn out, leading one Labour minister to describe the railways as "a poor bag of assets".

He was by no means wide of the mark, for by then none of the Big Four had the assets to tackle the maintenance and renewal backlog.

Many classes of ageing locomotives had avoided the cutter's torch because they would be needed for wartime service, and so by 1945, were in need of heavy repairs or direct replacement. The nation's ageing wagon fleet had in effect been run into the ground and passenger coaches, which had fallen off the bottom of the list of wartime priorities, had become shabby affairs.

While traffic levels, in particular freight, had soared from the day war had been declared, the rectification of wear and tear on the tracks had not followed suit. Indeed, track maintenance was, by 1945, running less than a third of prewar levels, and it was said that 2500 route miles needed attention.

The wartime government had limited railway earnings to £43.5 million per annum, and took whatever they earned above this amount – without investing any of it back into renewal and maintenance, although some of the surplus went into a fund for deferred postwar repairs.

It was clear to all that the parlous state of the system meant that the Big Four could not be returned to how they were before war broke out, let alone to the golden age of steam of the 1930s.

"Cheer Churchill – vote Labour" was the landslide election-winning slogan in

Labour's promises of a far better postwar world included permanent nationalisation of the railways.

1945. Promising a better world than the one in which servicemen coming home from the Western Front found in 1918, Clement Attlee's Labour government swept to power, and knew exactly how it would solve the problems besetting the worn-out railway network. Nationalise it, permanently.

And so, ending the debate, which had begun with William Galt's book and its influence on Gladstone in 1843, the 1947 Transport Act came into force on January 1, 1948 and British Railways came into being.

CHAPTER 2

THE PEOPLE'S
RAILWAY

In British railway history, January 1, 1948 was a seminal moment. It marked the great watershed between the railway of the steam age and the modern era yet to come, for it was on that day that state control of the national network, a temporary measure during wartime, finally became cast in stone.

LMS Stanier 'Black Five' No. 45292 in shiny new hand-painted BR black livery at Marylebone station in April 1948. A DOW COLLECTION

As in the aftermath of the Second World War, there was widespread public disdain for the 'old order' largely based on the British class system, and a growing demand for widespread social reform. After the Allies secured victory over Hitler's Germany in May 1945, Winston Churchill, prime minister in the wartime coalition, and deputy prime minister, Labour's Clement Attlee, wanted the arrangement to stay in place until Japan had also been beaten.

However, the coalition's Home Secretary, Herbert Morrison, who had been minister of transport during the 1929-31 Labour government, said that the Labour party would have none of it, and so Churchill was forced to call a general election.

Watershed moment: a LMS station employee displays a poster announcing the creation of British Railways.
DAILY HERALD ARCHIVE

The Beveridge Report of 1942, written by the Liberal economist William Beveridge, argued that maintenance of full employment would be the aim of postwar governments, and that this would provide the basis for the welfare state.

When released, it sold hundreds of thousands of copies, and in its wake, the three major parties committed themselves to such aims. However, the public saw Labour as the party most likely to deliver on the report's promises.

Labour campaigned on the theme of 'Let Us Face the Future' positioning itself as the party best placed to rebuild Britain after the war. By contrast, the Conservative campaign was based on Churchill, the hugely popular war hero, accordingly assuming that the election victory would be his. Indeed, newspapers predicted a clear Tory majority.

Here, I might draw parallels with the 2017 general election called by Prime Minister Theresa May with the expectation of a 50-seat majority, but while the Tories increased their share of the vote, a startling resurgence by Labour leader Jeremy Corbyn, a left-winger who by and large had been written off, made substantial gains and took away the Conservatives' overall majority.

Defeating Hitler was undoubtedly a monumental factor in Churchill's favour, but that was all now history. Yes, he had led Britain to victory against the Axis powers, but voters wondered if he could deliver sufficient change in peacetime.

Memories of the aftermath of the Second World War were still fresh in people's minds; many of the returning soldiers found little, if anything, had changed, and social conditions had not improved.

They had been promised Homes fit for Heroes, but while the vast programme on building council housing estates did much for the upper working classes, the poorer members of society in many cases remained forgotten, without a stake in the brave new world.

Churchill infamously accused Attlee, his former War Cabinet colleague, of seeking to behave as a dictator. In Churchill's first election broadcast on June 4, he stated that Labour, "would have to fall back on some form of a Gestapo" to inflict socialism on Britain.

The next night, Attlee thanked the prime minister for demonstrating to people the difference between Churchill the great wartime leader and Churchill the peacetime politician, and reinforced his case for state control of industry, including transport.

Labour Prime Minister, Clement Attlee, who presided over the nationalisation of major British industries including the railway network.

WINNING THE WAR, BUT LOSING THE PEACE

Attlee himself was taken by surprise at the size of his party's landslide victory when the results of the election were announced on July 26, 1945.

Labour had won 47.7% of the vote compared with Churchill's 36%, and the party was left with a working Commons majority of 146. The 12% national swing from the Conservative party to Labour remains the largest ever achieved in a British general election. Incidentally, in 2017, Labour's proportion of the vote grew by 9.6%, and saw the biggest swing since Attlee's landslide, although it was not enough to take Jeremy Corbyn into Number 10.

Attlee chose Herbert Morrison as his deputy prime minister, with overall responsibility for nationalisation. The new Labour government was committed to rebuilding British society as an ethical commonwealth, using public ownership and controls to abolish extremes of wealth and poverty.

His party's ideology contrasted sharply with the Conservative's defence of inherited privileges.

Labour's health minister, Aneurin Bevan, fought hard against the medical establishment, including the British Medical Association, to create

The British public was convinced that in 1945, the Labour Party offered the best hope for postwar prosperity.

LMS Fowler Beyer-Garratt 2-6-0+0-6-2T No. 7987, seen at Copmanthorpe in 1948, had not yet had its British Railways' number 47987 applied. E SANDERSON/COLOUR-RAIL

the National Health Service in 1948. This was a ground-breaking publicly funded healthcare system that offered treatment free of charge for all at the point of use.

Its need was no more illustrated by the fact that 8.5-million dental patients were treated and more than five million pairs of spectacles were issued during the first year of the NHS, highlighting the fact that a large slice of the population had been going without medical treatment rather than pay for it.

It has been said that there was more than a little influence from the railway sector in Bevan's blueprint for the NHS.

The Great Western Railway was in its early days not just years ahead of competitors in terms of transport technology, but also in terms of social conditions for its workforce.

GWR engineer, Isambard Kingdom Brunel, his locomotive superintendent, Daniel Gooch, and the company's directors showed a regard for their workers that was in its day as radical as their engineering exploits. They lived in an age where young children still worked in factories and mines and social conditions for the working classes in the new conurbations spawned by the Industrial Revolution were often low and life expectancy for certain trades such as slate mining notoriously short.

At Swindon, however, Gooch oversaw the building of a model village for his workers. Concerned for the moral and physical welfare of the men under him, he brought in a works doctor who stayed in free lodgings.

The workers' village was called 'New Swindon' and is today known

as the Railway Village. At the time it was separate from 'Old Swindon', but as the booming railway brought waves of prosperity and new inhabitants to the town, the two merged.

The Railway Village, one of the earliest examples of planned industrial housing in Britain, was designed by Sir Matthew Digby Wyatt, the architect of Paddington station. It comprised 300 limestone-built terraced houses, each with its own small front garden, in a series of six tree-lined wide parallel streets named after GWR stations,

Clement Attlee meeting King George VI after Labour's 1945 landslide election victory. When Attlee went to see the king at Buckingham Palace to be appointed prime minister, and told him: "I've won the election," the king replied: "I know. I heard it on the six o'clock news."

running from the east and west of a central square. Much of the stone for the houses came from the excavations of Box Tunnel.

New Swindon boasted three pubs and a church. St Mark's, which was built largely by public subscription and completed by 1845, with a graveyard where generations of local railwaymen found their final resting place within a stone's throw of Brunel's main line.

Next to the church was a school, built in 1845 for the children of GWR employees. Weekly fees were charged for the first four children of a family, but any more could go free.

At the heart of the village was the Mechanics' Institute, which has been described as Swindon's most important building, as well as being of great national importance.

Opened on May 1, 1855, it was funded by Gooch and works manager Minard Christian Rea's New Swindon Improvement Company, with the aim of providing evening classes for manual workers and their families.

Its library was the successor of one that had been set up in September 1843 by a small group of works employees, who the following year founded the GWR Mechanics' Institution, meeting in a room inside the works provided by the company for its first 11 years, until the showpiece premises of its own were opened. The library, with just 130 volumes in March 1844, predated the first council library in Britain, at Salford, which opened in 1852.

The Institute also had a theatre and stage, baths and coffee rooms. It served as a community centre, long before local authorities saw the need for such establishments to provide a focus for community life.

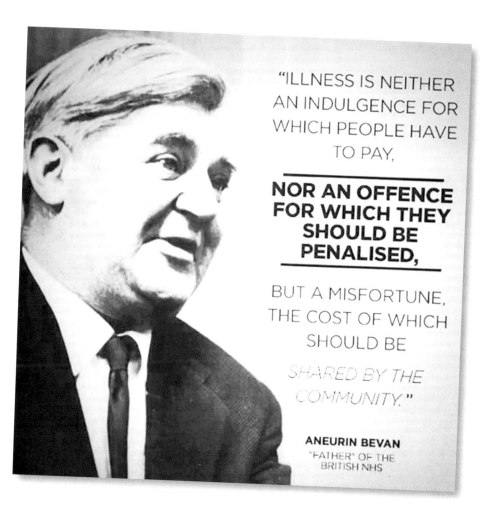

"ILLNESS IS NEITHER AN INDULGENCE FOR WHICH PEOPLE HAVE TO PAY,

NOR AN OFFENCE FOR WHICH THEY SHOULD BE PENALISED,

BUT A MISFORTUNE, THE COST OF WHICH SHOULD BE

SHARED BY THE COMMUNITY."

ANEURIN BEVAN
'FATHER' OF THE BRITISH NHS

Aneurin Bevan created the National Health Service, but did he draw his ideas from the Great Western Railway's Mechanics' Institution and its GWR Medical Fund Society healthcare programme?

BELOW: The Attlee government took mines into state ownership and created the National Coal Board. Many collieries had extensive railway systems, but these were not taken into the British portfolio but remained under the control of the NCB.

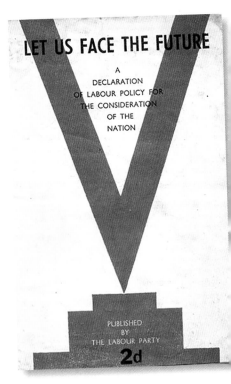

LET US FACE THE FUTURE

A DECLARATION OF LABOUR POLICY FOR THE CONSIDERATION OF THE NATION

PUBLISHED BY THE LABOUR PARTY

2d

Labour's 1945 manifesto for a brighter future in peacetime. The V echoed Churchill's famous Second World War 'V for Victory' sign.

The Institute also provided a marketplace in the Railway Village, making sure that workers could obtain a supply of fresh produce at reasonable prices.

A GWR Medical Fund Society was established that also financed a cottage hospital. In return for a small weekly deduction from their wages, employees and their families became entitled to a complete medical service, subsidised by the GWR.

It provided doctors' surgeries, dental and eye clinics, a casualty department and facilities for every branch of health service, from chiropody to the provision of artificial limbs.

This fund was a world first, which many believe, a century later would become a model for Aneurin Bevan when he designed the National Health Service. If that is so, Britain indeed has much to thank Swindon for, never mind the railway.

Attlee's government also created a 'cradle to grave' welfare state, with a new system of social security, legislation to build new towns and more homes, improved conditions for women and children, far better workers' rights including, among many, many other provisions, safeguarding the health and safety of people at work.

Attlee's government also carried out their manifesto commitment for nationalisation of basic industries and public utilities. The Bank of England and civil aviation were nationalised in 1946. Mining, railways, road haulage, canals, and Cable and Wireless were nationalised in 1947, with electricity and gas following in 1948.

The steel industry was nationalised in 1951, by which time around 20% of the British economy had been taken into public ownership.

Nationalisation brought major benefits for workers in the form of higher wages, shorter working hours, and improvements in working conditions. It did not, however, succeed in giving

North British-built LMS 'Jubilee' 4-6-0 No. 45572 at Chesterfield Midland in 1948.
D JENKINSON/COLOUR-RAIL

workers a greater say in the running of the industries in which they worked.

Within a few years of nationalisation, several progressive measures had been carried out that went a very long way to improving conditions in the mines, including better pay, a five-day working week, a national safety scheme, a ban on boys under the age of 16 going underground, the introduction of training for newcomers before going down to the coalface, and making pithead baths a standard facility.

After Labour's landslide victory in 1945, Clement Attlee chose Herbert Morrison as deputy prime minister, with overall responsibility for nationalisation. He had been minister of transport in what was Labour's second government between 1929-31.

GOODBYE BIG FOUR – HELLO BRITISH RAILWAYS

The new Labour government's proposals for bringing the country's inland transport services under public ownership were made known on November 28, 1946, when the full text of its Transport Bill was issued.

The Transport Act 1947 nationalised nearly all forms of mass transport in Britain and took effect from January 1, 1948.

The full title of the legislation was, 'An Act to provide for the establishment of a British Transport Commission concerned with transport and certain other related matters, to specify their powers and duties, to provide for the transfer to them of undertakings, parts of undertakings, property, rights, obligations and liabilities, to amend the law relating to transport, inland waterways, harbours and port facilities, to make certain consequential provision as to income tax, to make provision as to pensions and gratuities in the case of certain persons who become officers of the Minister of Transport, and for purposes connected with the matters aforesaid.'

In Northern Ireland, the Ulster Transport Authority acted in a similar manner.

The government also nationalised other means of transport such as canals, sea and shipping ports (but not coastal shipping), bus companies, and eventually, in the face of much opposition, long-distance road haulage. All of these transport modes, including

222 Marylebone Road, which became the first headquarters of British Railways. JOHN EDSER

Gresley A4 Pacific No. 4902 *Seagull,* by then given the number 60033 by British Railways, heads out of King's Cross in 1949. JF AYLARD/COLOUR-RAIL

British Railways, were brought under the control of a new body, the British Transport Commission, which was responsible to the Ministry of Transport.

The overall aim of the nationalisation of transport was to create a publicly owned centrally planned integrated system, with the BTC co-ordinating different modes of transport, so they worked hand-in-hand with each other instead of competing.

It all looked good in theory, but would it really stop the more versatile road transport squeezing railway lines out of business?

Sir Eustace Missenden on the footplate of his namesake, Southern Railway Bulleid 4-6-2 No. 34090 *Sir Eustace Missenden* on February 15, 1949.

TRANSPORT ACT 1947

GREAT WESTERN RAILWAY COMPANY
LONDON MIDLAND & SCOTTISH RAILWAY COMPANY
LONDON & NORTH EASTERN RAILWAY COMPANY
SOUTHERN RAILWAY COMPANY
LONDON PASSENGER TRANSPORT BOARD

Notice is hereby given that in pursuance of the above Act the Undertakings of the above named bodies vest in the British Transport Commission on 1st January, 1948, and that on and after the said date all Byelaws, Regulations and Notices published by any of the said bodies and in operation immediately before the said date and all tickets, consignment notes and other documents issued or used on and after the said date and which bear the name of any of the said bodies shall be deemed to be published and issued by and in the name of the Railway Executive or the London Transport Executive (as the case may be) constituted under the said Act.

BY ORDER

31st December, 1947

British Railways came into existence on January 1, 1948 as the business name of the Railway Executive of the BTC. At a stroke, after 25 years, the Big Four were no more.

The Railway Executive had been appointed in the summer of 1947, and soon moved into its headquarters at 222 Marylebone Road, London, which railwaymen nicknamed 'the Kremlin'. Its chairman was Sir Eustace Missenden, the last general manager of the Southern Railway.

Missenden accepted the offer of the chairmanship while privately intending to retire "before too long". Highly suspicious of civil servants and politicians, he did not sit easily in government circles, and other Railway Executive members did not respond eagerly to a man who had chaired a rival pre-Nationalisation company.

In 1949 British Railways named Bulleid Battle of Britain Pacific No. 34090 *Sir Eustace Missenden – Southern Railway*, to honour his personal contribution and to pay tribute to the war effort of the Southern Railway's employees. Missenden retired in 1951, and died in 1973.

FROM BIG FOUR TO NEARLY AS BIG SIX

Under the Railway Executive, the national network was organised into six regions:

- North Eastern Region – LNER lines in England north of Shaftholme Junction, Doncaster.
- Eastern Region – LNER lines south of Shaftholme Junction, Doncaster (this region was later amalgamated with the North Eastern Region) (2836 route miles), headquarters at Liverpool Street.
- London Midland Region – LMS lines in England and Wales (4993 route miles), headquarters at Euston.
- Scottish Region – LMS and LNER lines in Scotland (3730 route miles), headquarters in Glasgow.
- Southern Region – Southern Railway lines (2250 route miles), headquarters in Waterloo.
- Western Region – Great Western Railway lines (3782 route miles), headquarters at Paddington.

The top priority of the new British Railways Board was to repair the infrastructure of the railways damaged by bombing, clear the backlog of maintenance, and rectify losses in locomotives and rolling stock.

However, New Year's Day 1948 came and went and the immediate aftermath might well have gone unnoticed by railway staff. The network system changed little, and by and large was left to carry on as before Nationalisation, with little changes to the service, while usage increased. The renewal and repair of track and stations was completed by 1954.

RIGHT: A 1948 map showing the territory of the six regions.
THE RAILWAY MAGAZINE

BELOW: LMS Fairburn 2-6-2T No. 42198 at Waterloo on April 23, 1948, its new British Railways' lettering having been applied. COLOUR-RAIL

MAP OF BRITISH RAILWAYS BROAD OUTLINE OF REGIONS STAGE I

From 1949, the railways in Northern Ireland passed to the Ulster Transport Authority. The year before, Beyer-Peacock-built GNR(I) V class 4-4-0 No. 84 *Falcon* is seen in full flight at Portadown. AD HUTCHINSON/COLOUR-RAIL

Preserved Glasgow Subway Car No. 41. The underground system in Glasgow was not taken into the British Railways' portfolio. ROBIN JONES

STILL INDEPENDENT

As at the Grouping of 1923, several independent light railways and industrial railways, including colliery lines, which did not contribute significant mileage to the system, were not included in British Railways. Some were so small that they were not worth nationalising and may have been considered financial liabilities, having a short life expectancy.

These included the Ashover Light Railway (closed 1950), the Corringham Light Railway (closed to passengers 1952; became an industrial line), the Cannock Chase & Wolverhampton Railway (now Chasewater Railway in part), Derwent Valley Light Railway (closed 1981), Easingwold Railway (closed 1957), the Felixstowe Dock & Railway, the Festiniog Railway, the Harrington & Lowca Light Railway (closed 1973), Jarrow East End Light Railway, the Leighton Buzzard Light Railway, the Manchester Ship Canal Railway (last section closed in 2009), the Milford Haven Dock & Railway, the

LEFT: Laurel and Hardy were the VIP guests at the reopening of the Romney, Hythe & Dymchurch Railway to Dungeness in 1947. This world-famous 15in gauge pleasure railway was pressed into military service during the Second World War, with armour plating applied to steam locomotives so that this potentially vulnerable section of the Kent coast could be patrolled around the clock, and so played a part of the defence of the realm. However, it was one of several narrow gauge lines and minor railways that were not considered worthy of being taken into the new British Railways. ROBIN JONES COLLECTION

London Transport Museum's preserved 1938 tube train at its Acton depot. London Underground was not taken into British Railways' ownership at Nationalisation. ROBIN JONES

RIGHT: The Liverpool Overhead Railway, the first electric elevated city railway in the world, was omitted from Nationalisation in 1948.

Shares in the railway companies were exchanged for British Transport Stock, with a guaranteed 3% return chargeable to the British Transport Commission, and were repayable after 40 years.

Experts have claimed that because the government based the levels of compensation for railway shareholders on the valuation of their shares in 1946 (when the whole railway infrastructure was in a rundown and dilapidated state because of war damage and minimal maintenance) the railways were acquired comparatively cheaply.

That is a matter for debate, because others point out that even before the war, three of the Big Four companies were all but bankrupt, and were saved from declaring bankruptcy by the outbreak of hostilities in September 1939.

In that case, the exchange of potentially worthless private stock for government gilts based on a valuation during an artificially created boom might therefore be regarded as a very good deal.

The road haulage industry bitterly opposed Nationalisation, and found allies in the Conservative party. Once the Conservatives, under Winston Churchill, were re-elected in 1951, road haulage was soon privatised and deregulated, but railways and buses remained regulated, and were left under the control of the British Transport Commission.

Mumbles Railway & Pier (closed 1960), the North Sunderland Railway (closed 1951), the Nottingham Colwick Estates Light Railway, the Barrington Light Railway, the Ravenglass & Eskdale Railway, Romney Hythe & Dymchurch Railway, the Snailbeach District Tramways (closed 1950), the South Shields Marsden & Whitburn Colliery Light Railway, the Snowdon Mountain Railway, the Stocksbridge Railway, the Talyllyn Railway, the Trafford Park Railway (closed 1998), the Western Point Light Railway, the Wincham Light Railway, and the Wissington Light Railway (became British Sugar Corporation industrial line, 1957). Several of these were tourist lines and survive today as heritage railways.

London Underground and the Glasgow Subway, already both public concerns, were similarly excluded from the British Railways' portfolio, as were the Liverpool Overhead Railway, and non-railway-owned tramways, and military lines, such as the Longmoor Military Railway (although the Bicester Military Railway was already under government control).

The Northern Counties Committee lines owned by the LMS were sold to the Northern Ireland government, becoming part of the Ulster Transport Authority in 1949.

FAREWELL TO COMPETITION

The Railway Magazine of January/February 1947 commented: "The nationalisation of British railways will prove an even greater blow to the railway enthusiast than the grouping under the 1921 Act. Then 123 railways were merged into four, with the consequent elimination of much of the colour and many of the picturesque details, which had distinguished railways in Great Britain.

"Now it appears to be likely that even the four principal liveries to which the railways have been reduced, will be further standardised, and it may not be looking too far ahead to envisage a time when the predominant tone may be pillar-box red for the nationalised rolling stock.

"The final remnants of the competitive spirit between companies will be eliminated, and there is no reasonable prospect that the dull uniformity of standardisation will be offset by greater efficiency in operation."

British Railways' black-liveried LNER V2 2-6-2 No. 60835 at York in 1949. E SANDERSON/COLOUR-RAIL

Yet what would have been the likely outcome if Britain's railways had not been nationalised in the years of postwar austerity?

Would the Big Four, already heavily in debt in 1939, have been able to raise the money to make good the years of minimalist maintenance and war damage? Had they remained independent, it would have been likely that the Big Four would have needed colossal public subsidies to continue operations, even if there had been no meaningful programmes to replace tired locomotives and rolling stock.

Such a situation may well have led to far more closures of unprofitable routes, many years before anyone in the sector had heard of the name Beeching.

CHAPTER 3

GWR diesel railcar No. 4, a static exhibit inside the National Railway Museum at York. ROBIN JONES

STEAM'S
Last Blast

It was a foregone conclusion in 1948 that in the future, diesel and electric traction would replace steam locomotives, but just not yet. In the bleak years of postwar austerity, Britain could not afford an overwhelming investment in all-new railway infrastructure, so steam would be given one last blast, under Robert Riddles, a man who had worked with some of the country's greatest locomotive designers, as well as designing his own for the war effort.

The Second World War had left victorious Britain lagging well behind other countries in terms of railway modernisation.

During the Thirties, the USA and European countries had been introducing diesel and electric traction. On the far side of the Atlantic, diesel-electric locomotives came into widespread use following development of Electro-Motive Corporation's EA/EB design, first tested on the Baltimore & Ohio Railroad in 1937, however, for another two decades, Britain was still left in the steam age.

By comparison, Canadian Pacific ordered its first diesel in 1937, turned out its last new steam locomotive in 1949 and completed dieselisation by 1960. The Irish Republic, which had remained neutral during the war, introduced main line diesel railcars in 1950.

The first example of 'modern traction' in the UK may be said to have been a pair of experimental railcars built by the North Eastern Railway in York. These were powered by petrol engines, which generated electricity for two traction motors that were mounted on the bogie below. It was a pioneering principle and

Robert Riddles demonstrating the seated driving position in a Britannia Pacific mock-up.

Pioneer NER petrol-electric autocar No. 3170 undergoing restoration at Embsay on the Embsay & Bolton Abbey Railway. 1903 ELECTRIC AUTOCAR TRUST

one that would eventually be developed into the diesel-electric technology that powered and powers many locomotives worldwide. However, rival companies remained sceptical. The NER built no more 'autocars', so called because they could be driven from either end, as with modern passenger trains.

The railcars worked in Yorkshire on lines round Scarborough, Harrogate and Selby. No. 3171 was withdrawn on May 31, 1930 and No. 3170 on April 4, 1931.

The body of No. 3170 was used as a holiday home near Kirbymoorside in North Yorkshire for 70 years and was bought by acclaimed coach restorer Stephen Middleton in 2003. The 1903 Electric Autocar Trust was formed to restore the vehicle – to be powered by a new diesel engine – and a trailer coach

to form an Edwardian multiple unit. The Great Western Railway was the first British railway company to produce a fleet of diesel railcars. The official run of No. 1, the first of the fleet, took place from Paddington to Reading with a large number of press representatives present on December 1, 1933, and entered service three days later working from Slough shed to Windsor and Didcot.

In late 1947, the LMS unveiled Britain's first main line diesels, but at the time, they represented a lone voice crying in a steamy wilderness.

LMS Co-Cos Nos. 10000 and 10001 were built in association with English Electric at Derby Works, using an English Electric 1600hp diesel engine, generator and electrics. No. 10000 was officially presented to the press at

Derby Works in December 1947, and shortly afterwards at Euston station a week before Christmas, making a demonstration return journey to Watford. These Co-Cos were initially operated primarily on main line express passenger services.

Yes, the government and railway operators knew by the late Forties that mass dieselisation and electrification was inevitable, but broke Britain did not have anything like the necessary resources to make the leap.

A pragmatic decision was accordingly taken. For the present, steam would stay supreme, and the newly nationalised railway turned to a man who had begun his railway career as a Crewe Works apprentice in 1909 to head its postwar locomotive building policy.

Britain's first main line diesel locomotive, No. 10000, on trial through Chinley. Successful in service, it was years ahead of its time. When it appeared in the late Forties, war-weary Britain did not have enough money to replace steam with diesel and electric traction. As a result, the newly formed British Railways appointed a man who could hold the fort for steam.

An 1890 view of the erecting shop at the LNWR's Crewe Works, where Robert Riddles later became an apprentice.

THE LAST OF THE CHIEF MECHANICAL ENGINEERS

Robert 'Robin' Arthur Riddles, as Mechanical Engineer of British Railways, probably had more power than anyone else who had ever held a similar title in this country. Born on May 23, 1892, he joined the LNWR at Crewe Works as a premium apprentice in 1909, completing his apprenticeship in 1913.

While attending Mechanics Institute classes he took a course in electrical engineering, even at that early age believing that one day, the future of the railways would lie with electric traction.

Serving with the Royal Engineers in France during the First World War, he was badly injured. After the war ended, he was back at Crewe, where he oversaw the building of a new erecting shop.

Riddles was placed in charge of a small production progress department and was sent to Horwich to study the methods used by the Lancashire & Yorkshire Railway. The experience gained there was to prove helpful in furthering Riddles' career and he was to have significant influence in the reorganisation of Crewe Works, which took place between 1925-27, after the Grouping. In 1923 the LNWR had become part of the LMS and on completion of the work at Crewe, Riddles was sent to the former Midland Works at Derby to supervise a similar programme. He was supported in this process by Henry Ivatt who was the works manager at Derby.

During the General Strike of 1926, Riddles volunteered as a driver, taking trains from Crewe to Manchester and Carlisle. The experience he gained made him unique among Chief Mechanical Engineers and the practical knowledge gained at the coal face was of great assistance to Riddles in his future design work. For example, it was the difference experienced in driving a Prince of Wales 4-6-0 and a George the Fifth 4-4-0 that convinced Riddles of the advantage of six coupled wheels.

Riddles was a steam enthusiast and although he undoubtedly learned much from driving engines, equally he appears to have got quite a thrill from the experience.

William Stanier made him his Locomotive Assistant in 1933. Riddles moved to Euston, and graduated to Principal Assistant two years a later.

In this position, Riddles was responsible for much of the design work on Stanier's Princess Coronation Pacific. Riddles and Stanier developed a close relationship, and there is little doubt that this was of a great benefit to LMS locomotive design during the 1930s.

It has been alleged by some experts that Riddles was responsible for the design of the Princess Coronations and certainly Stanier was in India at the time of their construction, but others claim there is no evidence for this. However, Riddles did write about the infamous press run of streamlined Princess Coronation Pacific No. 6220 *Coronation* in 1937 and his description of events was particularly graphic.

That trip was the stuff of legend.

LNWR engine No. 819 Prince of Wales, which, outshopped in 1911, gave its name to a class that eventually numbered 245 and influenced Robert Riddles on locomotive design.

BROKEN CROCKERY A CAREER SETBACK?

Stanier's first prototype Pacific had been No. 6200 *The Princess Royal*, outshopped on June 27, 1933.

The official name for the class came about because Mary, the Princess Royal, was the Commander-in-Chief of the Royal Scots, and they were chosen to haul the LMS 'Royal Scot' train.

Combatting the challenge from the LNER, the LMS drew up plans for a six-hour non-stop service from Euston to Glasgow, the 'Coronation Scot'.

For a trial run, the senior driver from Crewe North shed, Tom Clark, was chosen to drive Princess Royal Pacific No. 6201 *Princess Elizabeth* from Euston to Glasgow Central, assisted by fireman, Charles Fleet.

On November 16, 1936, the train covered London to Glasgow in five hours 53mins 38secs. The next day, the non-stop return journey was made in five hours 44mins 14secs, at an average speed of 69mph, with an average load of 240 tons. It was another steam watershed, and Clark and his crew were feted as the pop stars of the day by the national press.

A bigger version of the Princess Royals, the Princess Coronation class comprised 38 of the most powerful passenger steam locomotives ever built for Britain's railways,

Their tenders were fitted with a steam-operated coal pusher to supply fuel to the firing plate, helping fireman tackle the 299-mile non-stop run from Euston to Carlisle on the 'Royal Scot'.

Countering the public relations value of the streamlined A4s, the first five Princess Coronations, Nos. 6220-4, were fitted with an art deco air-smoothed casing and painted Caledonian Railway blue with silver horizontal lines to match the 'Coronation Scot' train.

Driver Tom Clark was again selected to handle what would be spectacular run, in a bid to snatch back the world steam record from the LNER.

On the fabled press trip of Tuesday, June 29, 1937, preceding the launch of the 'Coronation Scot' Clark's crew took the first of the Princess Coronations, No. 6220 Coronation, the 158 miles from Euston to Crewe in two hours 9mins 45secs, with a top speed of 114mph, claimed just south of Crewe.

Clark did not take into account the necessary braking distance before entering a series of crossover points on the approach to Crewe, and took the 20mph approach curve at 52mph, resulting in the crockery in the train's dining car famously crashing to the floor.

Riddles was on board the locomotive at the time that the train was travelling at up 70mph when it approached the Crewe platform signal. However, Clark managed to bring the train to a standstill at the station – a testament both to him,

The first streamlined Princess Coronation Pacific, No. 6220 *Coronation*, hauls the 'Coronation Scot' on its test run in 1937. But did Robert Riddles' graphic report on its 'misdemeanour' on the approach to Crewe damage his career prospects?

his crew and Stanier's locomotive design. Going back to Euston from Crewe, the 119 minute-trip was covered at an average speed of 79.7mph, one of the fastest-ever recorded in Britain. However, the LMS and the LNER agreed, for the sake of safety concerns, not to do any more high-speed runs for publicity purposes.

Less than a month after claiming the world speed record, on July 12, 1937 Tom Clark drove the Royal Train from Crewe to Euston, where King George VI presented him with an OBE for his record run the previous year.

This vivid description of the train achieving a speed of 114 mph much

too close to Crewe station for comfort is considered to have damaged Riddles' prospects within the LMS. As well as the smashed crockery, there was also some damage to the points, but Riddles treated it as a great adventure.

In 1937 he moved to Glasgow as the LMS Mechanical and Electrical Engineer for Scotland, at the same time that Charles Fairburn was appointed as Stanier's deputy – much to Riddles' disappointment – this backward step in his career could have been partly down to the result of the *Coronation* episode.

THE SECOND WORLD WAR

In 1939 with the Second World War having just started, Riddles moved to the Ministry of Supply, becoming director of transportation equipment, in which position he is credited with his first locomotive designs; the War Department Austerity 2-8-0 and 2-10-0s.

The Ministry of Supply had adopted the Stanier 8F 2-8-0 as the War Department's standard type and the three other Big Four companies joined in their production, but they were expensive. In 1942 during the early planning stages for the invasion of Europe, it was realised that large numbers of main line and shunting locomotives would have to be built and used on both British and European lines.

What was needed was something that could be produced in quantity, cheaply and quickly. Riddles' WD 2-8-0 was the answer.

The 2-8-0 was quite a tidy design for an 'austerity' locomotive but the taper boiler and Belpaire firebox of the 8F was replaced by a parallel boiler and round-topped firebox, while castings and forgings were replaced by fabrication.

The railway companies knew that they would inherit the WD engines once hostilities had ceased, and would have much preferred these to be Stanier 8Fs than Riddles' ones, but for now, it was the 'Austerities' that they were instructed to build.

When Riddles went on to produce his 2-10-0 version, it was with the variation of a wide firebox rather than the narrow

Princess Coronation Pacific No. 6229 *Duchess of Hamilton* masquerading as No. 6220 *Coronation* departs Hartford, Connecticut, on the New York, New Haven & Hartford Railroad during its 1939 US tour. Robert riddles drove the celebrity locomotive for much of the tour. THE RAILWAY MAGAZINE

RIDDLES' AMERICAN ADVENTURE

Coronation may have stolen the headlines, but a sister locomotive took its place – and identity – for a prestigious transatlantic trip.

No. 6229 *Duchess of Hamilton*, which was built at Crewe in 1938 as the 10th member of its class, became "No. 6220 Coronation" – and along with a complete 'Coronation Scot' train comprising three articulated pairs of coaches, a sleeping car and a club car, represented the LMS at the New York World's Fair in 1939-40.

It was not the first time that the LMS had sent a locomotive with another's identity to the USA.

In 1933 No. 6152 *The King's Dragoon Guardsman* was sent to the Century of Progress International Exposition in Chicago as class doyen No. 6100 *Royal Scot*, and kept that identity after it returned to the UK.

For the World's Fair, No. 6229 was chosen because at the time it was the most recent locomotive to come out of Crewe.

The central theme of the fair was the future, with an opening slogan of, "Dawn of a New Day", and it set out to showcase, "the world of tomorrow".

So the LMS decided to exhibit its most modern train to the rest of the world.

The identity exchange left a blue-liveried 'No. 6229 Duchess of Hamilton' running in Britain, and a crimson lake 'Coronation' in North America.

To comply with US railroad laws, 'No. 6220' was fitted with a huge headlamp and brass bell along with brackets for side lamps and a claw coupling. None of the other LMS streamliners ever had such features.

The tour train ran from Crewe to Euston where it was publicly unveiled on January 9, 1939. The train including 'Coronation' was hauled from Willesden to Southampton Docks and loaded aboard the Norwegian *MV Belpamela*, which was specially designed for shipping railway vehicles, and sailed on January 26. The ship arrived in Baltimore on February 20.

The train was unloaded four days later, and taken to the Baltimore & Ohio Railroad's workshops at Mount Clare for the locomotive to be reassembled.

A private test run was followed by an unveiling to a VIP audience in the workshops on March 17, with a press run

to Washington and back the next day. The train made a 3121-mile tour of the USA, hosted by the Baltimore & Ohio Railroad, as a build-up to the World's Fair.

The tour began on March 21, with the starting signal being electrically activated directly from the fairground.

During most of the tour of North America, Riddles drove the locomotive after the nominated driver, Fred Bishop, fell ill. As with the 1937 speed run, Riddles also described this trip with great enthusiasm and in vivid detail, and indeed, Fred Bishop was very complimentary about Riddles' driving skills.

The tour was a massive success, with 'Coronation' aka *Duchess of Hamilton* attracting crowds wherever it went. It was estimated that around 425,000 people came on board at the stations to inspect the luxurious interior, and two million people saw it at the fair itself.

The grand opening of the fair took place on Sunday, April 30, the 150th anniversary of George Washington's inauguration as President in New York City.

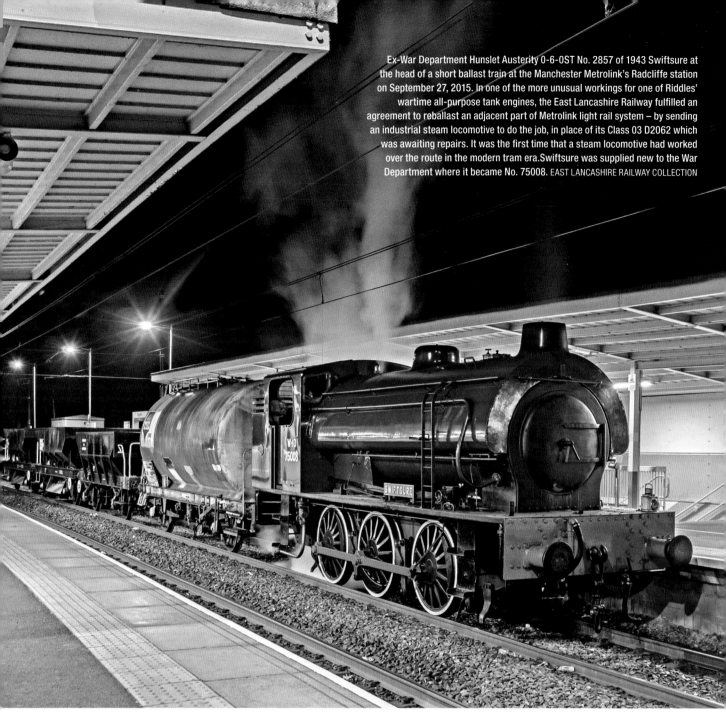

Ex-War Department Hunslet Austerity 0-6-0ST No. 2857 of 1943 Swiftsure at the head of a short ballast train at the Manchester Metrolink's Radcliffe station on September 27, 2015. In one of the more unusual workings for one of Riddles' wartime all-purpose tank engines, the East Lancashire Railway fulfilled an agreement to reballast an adjacent part of Metrolink light rail system – by sending an industrial steam locomotive to do the job, in place of its Class 03 D2062 which was awaiting repairs. It was the first time that a steam locomotive had worked over the route in the modern tram era. Swiftsure was supplied new to the War Department where it became No. 75008. EAST LANCASHIRE RAILWAY COLLECTION

firebox of the 2-8-0. Despite the desire to reduce costs and steam on poor-quality coal, copper was still available for all the 2-8-0s, but the 2-10-0s' fireboxes were steel. Surprisingly, the two types were of virtually identical power, although the 2-10-0s had much better adhesion; the 2-8-0s being surprisingly poor in this respect.

Riddles designed three very successful 'Austerity' designs. As well as the 2-8-0 and 2-10-0, there was the Hunslet-based 0-6-0ST, produced to meet the projected shunting needs. The first of these saddle tanks was steamed in January 1943, and a total of 377 were built for the War Department over the next four years.

These were designed to be cheap and easy to build and maintain, and to burn indifferent coal. They also proved powerful for their size, and could run on poor-quality track. In 1944, a number were loaned to the Ministry of Fuel and

A WD Austerity 2-10-0 at work in Scotland in 1944. Riddles' 2-10-0s were the first type with this wheel arrangement to run in Britain, and the country's first major class of 10-coupled engines. In this respect and more, they paved the way for Riddles' BR Standard 9Fs, which many believe were the finest steam locomotives ever produced in Britain. His 2-10-0s were designed to have interchangeable parts with his 2-8-0s. THE RAILWAY MAGAZINE

Power for working various open-cast coal sites.

The railway companies were given the responsibility of maintaining these locomotives, and the LNER became responsible for 25 of these engines in January 1945. Impressed by their rugged design, the LNER purchased 75 locomotives and gave them the classification of J94.

The order was placed in May 1946 and most were quickly delivered in June and July of 1946. With the shortage of materials in postwar Britain, the purchase of the J94s was clearly preferable to building new J50s for the LNER's heavy shunting requirements.

As time was of the essence, Riddles adapted the standard Hunslet 18in inside-cylinder industrial 0-6-0ST,

incorporating a variety of austerity features.

All three of Riddles' WD designs were used extensively in the UK and in Europe. The LNER used many of the 0-6-0STs (Class J94) and 2-8-0s during and after hostilities.

It was also the LNER that obtained the 2-8-0s in large numbers after the war, classifying them O7. They were,

War Department heavy freight 2-8-0 No. 90733 with a goods train at Oakworth on the Keighley & Worth Valley Railway. BRIAN SHARPE

of course, inherited by BR and the 732 engines gave good service on slow, heavy freight traffic almost to the end of steam. BR did eventually get the opportunity to purchase 25 of the 2-10-0s, which found work in Scotland. It has been said that Riddles was anxious to get back into the railway business proper, as opposed to his work for the Ministry of Supply. In 1943 he moved to

the post of chief stores superintendent at the LMS, and on Charles Fairburn's death in 1944 he applied for the position of Chief Mechanical Engineer, but this time the job went to George Ivatt, with Riddles being promoted to vice-president of the LMS.

POSTWAR PROMOTION

On the creation of the Railway Executive in 1947 in preparation for Nationalisation in 1948, Riddles was appointed a member of the Railway Executive for mechanical and electrical engineering.

He had two principal assistants, both of whom were also former LMS men: Roland C Bond, chief officer (locomotive construction and maintenance), and E S Cox, executive officer (design).

The duties of these three effectively covered the old post of Chief Mechanical Engineer.

In this new post, Riddles was able to take the decision to continue the construction of steam locomotives, on the basis that it was not worth changing to diesel traction when the ultimate aim was electrification.

His selection of two colleagues from the LMS as his assistants rather than men from Swindon, Eastleigh or Doncaster, clearly meant that LMS thinking would predominate when it came to BR steam locomotive design.

Riddles was responsible for organising the Locomotive Exchanges of 1948, as described in the next chapter.

These exchanges occurred at a time when the two aforementioned LMS diesels were already starting to prove themselves in service.

Henry George Ivatt, who had supervised their introduction and been part of the decision by the LMS to pursue dieselisation of main line services, was still involved as Chief Mechanical Engineer of that company's successor, the London Midland Region, and must have had grave misgivings about the direction being taken by Riddles, with whom he had worked for many years.

However, Riddles' bias towards Derby and Crewe was by no means a bad move, for under H G Ivatt, the LMS had done more to produce engine types that could be used anywhere in the country, and had adapted designs to suit postwar conditions. Ivatt had built very much on the foundations laid down by Stanier, who himself was a pupil of the GWR's George Jackson Churchward, so the lineage of the new British Railways' locomotives to come in many respects had roots in to Edwardian times.

A striking blue livery was adopted for express locomotives in the early years of British Railways. Here, LMS Duchess 4-6-2 No. 46241 waits at Camden in April 1949. W BOOT/COLOUR RAIL

BACK TO BLACK

Riddles had another major influence on the appearance of the post-Nationalisation steam fleet, which was never fully documented. As well as designing a new generation of steam locomotives, he had the task of establishing a 'standard' livery for BR's steam fleet.

Roland Bond, one of his deputies, was ex-Derby and favoured red. However, Riddles was a Crewe man, brought up on the LNWR; he was in charge and took the oft-quoted Henry Ford view that you can have "any colour you like as long as it is black".

After he set to work on the new colour scheme, engines were quickly painted in various possible liveries, mostly green, and paraded in front of the BR executive at Marylebone. They were mostly LMS 5MT 4-6-0s and not exactly in showroom condition. At the end of the performance though, Riddles admitted that he had

prepared another engine if the chairman would be interested, but it was not green, nor had this particular scheme even been considered.

Another LMS 5MT appeared, which Crewe had turned out in immaculate fully lined LNWR black. It stole the show, and Riddles is quoted as saying: "I got more than 19,000 out of 20,000 locomotives painted black, which was what I had wanted all along!"

Although blue was adopted for express engines, and Brunswick green for exclusively passenger engines, even Riddles' first Britannia Pacific, No. 70000 *Britannia*, was initially turned out in plain black, and Princess Coronation Pacifics were seen in black with LNWR-style lining for a while.

RIGHT: LMS Stanier 'Black Five' 4-6-0 No. 304611 with British Railways on the side, pictured at York in 1948. COLOUR-RAIL

CHAPTER 4

A passenger train crosses the Afon Dyfi bridge early in the 20th century. CRS

CORRIS:
An early closure

One of the first closures of a route by British Railways was that of the quaint Corris Railway, a rural outpost in central Wales, which succumbed a few months after Nationalisation.

A Corris Railway train at the line's northern passenger terminus of Aberllefenni in 1930. CRS

A popular yet erroneous general public misconception has it that railway closures were invented by Dr Richard Beeching, but as the ownership of motor transport became more widespread, the days of lines with comparatively low loadings, both in terms of passengers and freight, were numbered.

Lines built under the 1896 Light Railways Act were particularly at risk. The Act, which predated the emergence of car ownership by only a few years, allowed for minimalist country branches to be built on the cheap, with basic stations, secondhand locomotives and carriages as well as track with a 25mph speed limit, in order to enfranchise the small towns and villages that the major railway companies did not consider economically viable.

The Thirties saw a wave of semi-closures in the form of withdrawal of passenger services from some lines, although in many cases freight continued on such routes into the Fifties and Sixties. For example, the LMS Harborne branch in Birmingham lost its passenger services in 1934, although freight lingered on until 1963. Its trackbed is now a walkway, but what a boon it would be to today's heavily congested city if it could have been saved or if it was reopened?

Other Thirties casualties involving closures to passengers included the Southern Railway's Appledore Junction to New Romney branch in 1937, the LMS Derby to Langley Mill via Ripley branch (1930), the Grassington branch (1930) the LNER's Melmerby to Masham, via West Tanfield line (1931) and the Durham to Sunderland, via Hetton and Ryhope Junction (1931), to name but a few.

It was in that decade that several of the UK's most famous narrow gauge lines were closed. The Campbeltown & Machrihanish Light Railway in Scotland closed in 1932, the Leek & Manifold Valley Light Railway shut in 1934, and was followed the next year by the Lynton & Barnstaple Railway, and in 1936 by the Welsh Highland Railway. Closures and service withdrawals were taking place in the last year of the Big Four.

The Southern Railway's 16-mile Elham Valley line from Canterbury West to Folkestone West was closed completely in 1947, while the LMS Wirksworth branch from Duffield lost its passenger services. In modern times, it has been reopened as the Ecclesbourne Valley Railway. The GWR's very rural Alcester to Bearley line via Great Alne lost its passenger services, with freight ceasing four years later in 1951.

At Nationalisation there may have been many who thought that state control would halt or even reverse line closures and services losses. History, however, records that that was far from

An early 20th-century view of the new Corris Railway station and company offices at Machynlleth, following their completion in 1907. CRS

being the case, for closures continued in the first year of state ownership.

The first official closure under British Railways was the goods-only line from Mantle Lane East to the foot of Swannington Incline in Leicestershire, by the new London Midland Region, in February 1948. The first passenger services to be withdrawn were those from Woodford & Hinton station on the Great Central route, to Byfield on the Stratford & Midland Junction Railway, on May 31, 1948, also by the LMR.

On August 13, 1948, in the Scottish borders, the day after large-scale flooding took out the bridge over the River Teviot at Nisbet, the LNER Roxburgh Junction to Jedburgh via Nisbet and Jedfoot branch was closed to passengers, although goods traffic remained until August 10, 1964.

A week later, floods would seal the fate of an even more obscure outpost of the national network, in the form of the 2ft 3in gauge Corris Railway in central Wales, which would close completely.

Selwyn Humphries, whose late father, Humphrey, had driven the last Corris Railway train on August 20, 1948, in the cab of the new No. 7 at Corris station 57 years later. PETER GREENHOUGH/CRS

Reversing the withdrawal of passenger services under the GWR and the complete line closure under British Railways: the first official steam-hauled passenger train in the 21st century departs from Corris on August 20, 2005.
PETER GREENHOUGH/CRS

No. 4 with a goods train on the Afon Dyfi bridge in the late 1940s. The flooding of the river in 1948 and the subsequent track damage led to the immediate closure of the Corris Railway. CRS

FLOODS HELP CLOSE AN UNWANTED ANTIQUE?

The origins of the Corris Railway go back 1850, with the emergence of proposals to building a line to link slate quarries in the district around Corris, Corris Uchaf and Aberllefenni with wharves on the estuary of the Afon Dyfi at Derwenlas and Morben, south-west of Machynlleth, replacing a far less-efficient practice of using horse-drawn carts and sledges to make the same journey over poor muddy roads.

The 2ft 3in gauge Corris Machynlleth & River Dovey Tramroad opened on April 1, 1859. Locomotives were banned, so the tramway was worked as a horse-and-gravity-worked operation, taking slate from the quarries of Corris Uchaf and Aberllefenni to the nearest navigable point on the Afon Dyfi for it to be loaded on to ships.

With the coming of the standard gauge Newtown & Machynlleth Railway to Machynlleth in January 1863, the Corris line carried its slate to the town station's transhipment sidings rather than to the wharves further down the Dyfi estuary.

The owners of the narrow gauge line applied on November 13, 1863 to convert the tramroad to a railway and formally close the section between Machynlleth and Derwenlas, and on July 25, 1864 an Act of Parliament was passed changing the name to the Corris Railway Company and permitting the use of locomotives.

By the 1870s, a semi-official passenger service using wagons with wooden planks had taken off. The line was acquired by a London company, Imperial Tramways Ltd, in 1878. Three steam locomotives from the Hughes Locomotive & Tramway Engine Works Ltd at Falcon Works in Loughborough (which later evolved into the Brush Electrical Engineering Company) and 10 passenger carriages were introduced, although passenger services were suspended for another five years after a dispute with the quarry owners, who objected that passenger trains would interfere with their mineral traffic.

In 1880 and 1883, two new Acts were obtained that adjusted the tolls on the railway and allowed the carriage of passengers. The railway ran a test passenger service on local roads, and it became so successful that it was possible to pass the Parliamentary Act despite the opposition of the quarry owners. At first, passenger services ran between Machynlleth to Corris, with new stations at Esgairgeiliog and Llwyngwern opening in 1884. The track was upgraded beyond Corris so that passenger services could reach the line's northern terminus at Aberllefenni, with services commencing on August 25, 1887. Also that year, stations were also opened at Ffridd Gate and Garneddwen.

The takeover was seen to be a sound business move, for tourist traffic on the line took off in a big way. The railway was promoted as the best route to Tal-y-llyn Lake and Cader Idris, despite the presence of the rival Talyllyn.

The railway developed its own network of horse-hauled road services, including a link between Corris station and Abergynolwyn station on the Talyllyn, as part of a circular Grand Tour encompassing the two narrow gauge railways and the Cambrian main line service between Tywyn and Machynlleth.

THE ROT SETS IN

As on similar rural backwater lines elsewhere, the slate industry declined in the early 20th century, while road transport presented stiffening competition. A severe blow to the railway came in 1906 when Braichgoch Quarry closed, and although the line continued to serve the quarries around Corris and Aberllefenni, and hauled timber from the Dyfi forest, it never again made a profit. As well as slate and passengers, the line hauled timber extracted from the Dyfi forest in the 1910s through to the 1930s.

By then, Imperial Tramways had not only moved to Bristol, sharing offices and management with Bristol Tramways, but was successfully running its own bus services. Bristol motorbuses were dispatched to Corris to take over the road services. The Great Western Railway, which had pioneered the use of motorbus services and even used them to compete with its own branch lines, bought the Corris Railway in 1930, withdrawing passenger services at the beginning of the following year, and concentrating on the buses.

The line continued in use for freight use until 1948, when the newly nationalised British Railways took it over.

That year, the Afon Dyfi flooded and caused serious erosion to the bridge near Machynlleth. At the same time, the two remaining locomotives, Hughes 0-4-2 saddle tank No. 3 and Kerr Stuart Tattoo class 0-4-2 saddle tank No. 4, were in need of major overhauls.

The last train ran on Friday, August 20, 1948, and following floods over the next weekend, an inspection ruled it was not safe to continue operating trains. A lorry was brought in to take the quarried slate out instead, and official closure was confirmed in the following month. By the end of 1949 the track had been lifted.

The two locomotives remained in their shed at Machynlleth, where stationmaster, Campbell Thomas, hoped they would find their way to the Talyllyn, which had remained in private hands, and the Corris, which was also built to the very rare 2ft 3in gauge, so bought many of the lifted railways from its sister line.

It was to be a case of making two poor railways into one good one. In 1951, the newly formed Talyllyn Railway Preservation Society bought the two locomotives for £50 for the pair, along with several goods wagons and lengths of track. With repairs needed to their line's Fletcher Jennings 0-4-0WT No. 2 *Dolgoch*, the Talyllyn revivalists needed another locomotive, and where else could one built to 2ft 3in gauge be found?

At their new home, Corris No. 3 became *Sir Haydn* and No. 4 *Edward Thomas*, retaining their Corris numbers in the Talyllyn fleet.

No. 7 hauls its replica Corris train through the spinney north of Maespoeth. RICHARD GREENHOUGH/CRS

In 1958, the Talyllyn volunteers retrieved the remains of a Corris bogie carriage, which had been used as a summerhouse in Gobowen. It was rebuilt and returned to service, allowing a genuine Corris train to be formed by adding the surviving bake van to this coach and either of the locomotives.

So, the Corris had something of a second life, 'absorbed' into its one-time rival sister line.

Parts of the Corris system did remain in use despite the official closure by British Railways. The quarry at Ratgoed, inaccessible by road continued to use its horse-drawn tramway until 1952, while the last-remaining length of the railway proper, linking the Aberllefenni Quarry to the cutting sheds in the village, remained in use until the late 1970s, with a tractor pulling the wagons. Even when this fell into disuse, the underground section of track continued to be used.

Much of the rest of the line, devoid of track, returned to nature. However, just as some FFestiniog supporters had begun looking at the Welsh Highland as a possibility for revival, so some Talyllyn volunteers from the East Midlands began wondering if anything could be done for the Corris.

Obstacles to complete restoration had begun to appear. Council houses were built on the site of Aberllefenni station in the early Sixties, and the railway's yard at Machynlleth became used for warehousing. Meanwhile, some householders at Corris and Ffridi Gate had extended their gardens across the trackbed without telling British Railways, which remained the landowner.

GREENS SHOOTS FOR A FRESH SPRING
In December 1966 a group of enthusiasts led by Alan Meaden founded the Corris Railway Society with the aim of preserving what was left of the line,

opening a dedicated museum, and perhaps reviving part of the route. In the initial stages, a demonstration horse-drawn tramway was considered.

Corris station was demolished in 1968, but the society was subsequently able to obtain use of the adjacent railway stables at an affordable price. It was extensively repaired and in 1970 opened as the Corris Railway Museum. A short length of demonstration track was laid in 1971.

During the Seventies, the society continued fundraising while holding talks with the relevant authorities about reopening part of the line to passengers.

A new Corris Railway Company, reviving the original name, was incorporated to act as the society's trading and operating arm, while the society achieved charitable status.

In 1981, the railway's original locomotive shed at Maespoeth was acquired and became its operational base. Basic track was laid over a very modest three quarters of a mile between Maespoeth and Corris, and on April 20, 1985, Corris Railway No. 5, a Simplex Motor Rail four-wheeled diesel named Alan Meaden, in honour of the society's founder, hauled a rake of wagons and

formed the official 'first train' back to Corris in 1985, witnessed by former Corris Railway workers.

Following this landmark, the track was upgraded to passenger standards. In the autumn of 1996, former Corris locomotive No. 4 made a brief loan visit from the Talyllyn to celebrate its 75th anniversary.

Corris passenger trains finally ran again, after a 72-year gap, at 11am on June 3, 2002.

The final legal agreement needed to run trains – approval by the Strategic Rail Authority as the original Corris Railway was part of the British Railways network – arrived in time for the Spring bank holiday weekend.

The first official train comprised industrial Ruston Hornsby four-wheeled diesel No. 6, which was built in 1966 – the year that the Corris Railway Society was formed – the railway's single coach and a guard's van, the total passenger stock currently available.

The train was waved away by local landowner, Mrs Eluned Lloyd, whose farm is bisected by the railway and who, along with her late husband, has been praised for helping its revival. Staff from the Talyllyn Railway postal service travelled on board to issue first-day covers to mark the occasion.

However, the first public train to carry passengers had been run at 2pm on June 1, the same day that the line was cleared for public liability insurance. Services were run over all four days of the weekend, and were said to be mostly full. Each round trip took just 45mins.

The following year, the Corris Railway marked the 150th anniversary of its enabling Act of Parliament, by holding an official reopening weekend on June 7-8.

The Talyllyn loaned its complete heritage Corris train, comprising No. 3 Sir Haydn, coach No. 17, which was previously Corris No. 7, and original Corris brake van No. 6.

No. 3, which had hauled the last train on the original line in 1948, was also celebrating its 12th anniversary.

Before its temporary transfer for June, the locomotive was repainted at

Swannington Incline, the scene of the first British Railways closure in February 1948, is now under the supervision of the Swannington Heritage Trust and the trackbed down the incline has been opened as a footpath with information boards. The foundations of the engine house at the top of the incline have been uncovered and about 75yds of track laid have been relaid as a monument. The Leicester and Swannington Railway (L&S) was one of England's first railways, being opened on July 17, 1832 to bring coal from collieries in west Leicestershire to Leicester. ROBIN JONES

Pendre works in Indian Red, as near as possible to its original Corris livery.

The heritage train was booked to run regular timetable services back on its original line on every weekend throughout June, returning to Tywyn at the end of the month. While at Corris, locomotive crews were provided by the Talyllyn with a conductor/driver from Corris Railway Society on the footplate.

The 'old' Corris train ran in tandem with the 'new' one, comprising No. 6, and two near-replica 19th-century Corris carriages built by volunteers, Nos. 20 and 21. Unveiled at the reopening, No. 21 was the first new bogie carriage to be delivered to the Corris Railway since the Metropolitan Railway Car & Wagon Company Ltd supplied two vehicles in 1898.

Throughout the opening weekend, two steam services alternated with two diesel services, in order to give every visitor the chance to ride on one of each.

Corris No. 4 is now No. 4 *Edward Thomas* on the nearby sister line the Talyllyn Railway. It is ironic that two locomotives from this very early British Railways' line closure survived, while thousands of others from the nationalised network in later years ended up in scrapyards. ROBIN JONES

A NEW CORRIS STEAM LOCOMOTIVE

Society members stepped up several gears after accepting that there would never be a chance of buying one of the two surviving original Corris locomotives back from the Talyllyn, where they had become inextricably woven into the legend that is the Tywyn operation. The only course of action was to build their own.

Since the mid-Seventies, many new-build projects have been started by preservationists, by far the best known being the A1 Steam Locomotive Trust's Peppercorn A1 Pacific No. 60163 *Tornado*. The aim is normally the filling of missing gaps in the heritage-era locomotive fleet by recreating extinct locomotives.

In the case of the Corris new-build project, it was to create a replica Kerr Stuart Tattoo class locomotive as a substitute for the original No. 4.

An appeal for funds to build the new locomotive was launched in 1994, and detailed discussions begun with Winson Engineering of Daventry to build the engine.

The new locomotive, No. 7 in the Corris fleet, was the first all-new steam engine to be built for service in the UK on the rare 2ft 3in gauge since No. 4 was delivered new to the original railway in 1921.

One point, decided early on, was that the new Corris No. 7 would not be a slavish replica of No. 4, but a modern interpretation. So, while remaining as visually similar as possible to No. 4 in its Corris days, improvements made to the prototype by the Talyllyn could be incorporated.

No. 7 was built in stages in Daventry, with the contract for each part of the work being placed as funds were raised. The manufacturer getting into

financial difficulties in 2001 proved only a temporary problem, with arrangements made for construction to continue nearby.

It was on April 4, 2005 that No. 7 had its first official steaming in Daventry, for the benefit of the boiler inspector, who gave his approval. Soon afterwards it was moved to Tamworth for painting and lining out, at the private Statfold Barn Railway.

On May 17, 2005, No. 7 arrived at its new home at Corris. The project had cost £120,000. On May 27, it hauled a train carrying the Welsh Assembly's First Minister Rhodri Morgan over the railway.

When No. 7 hauled a public passenger train for the first time, the 11am from Corris on Saturday August 20, of that year, it was 57 years to the day since the final (freight) train ran on the original line. Among those present was Selwyn Humphries, whose late father Humphrey drove that last train in 1948.

Coun Gretta Jones of Gwynedd County Council and Corris Community Council cut a ribbon to send the steam service on its way, after giving a speech in which she praised the volunteer efforts in rebuilding the railway. In keeping with an old Corris Railway tradition, the train departed about 10mins late.

The railway has consolidated its facilities at Maespoeth with the construction of a new two-road carriage shed in a nearby field, the original carriage sheds at Corris and Machynlleth having been demolished.

During 2009 the railway marked the 150th anniversary of the first train on the Corris with a series of events, including demonstration horse-worked freight trains and gravity runs of rakes of wagons. While many people would undoubtedly like to see the railway

The first official service train hauled by new Kerr Stuart Tattoo No. 7 leaves Corris on August 20, 2005. PETER GREENHOUGH/CRS

rebuilt in its entirety, the society has long accepted more modest ambitions. At present, the railway is looking to extend southwards towards Machynlleth, with the initial aim of extending the line to the Forestry Commission car park at Tan-y-Coed, midway between Esgairgeiliog and Llwyngwern two-and-a-half miles south of Corris.

The trackbed is owned by the supportive Gwynedd County Council, which has agreed to sell it to the line once a Transport & Works Order is granted, and discussions about a further extension southwards from Tan-y-Coed are also taking place: a link to the Centre for Alternative Technology has also been mooted.

Back in 1948, the Corris Railway was written off in the wake of Nationalisation. Even if it had not been dealt a body blow by the floods, it is certain that British Railways would sooner rather than later have found a way of closing it.

However, taking its revival into account, the Corris may have been one of the earliest victims of British Railways' closures, but can count itself as one of the lucky ones, for many, many other rural lines would not be so fortunate in the decades ahead.

LED BY **IWM**

The LMS-Patriot Project

CREATING THE NEW NATIONAL MEMORIAL ENGINE

RAISING THE PRESSURE!

As many of you will be aware we received a setback when our supplier decided to end all sub-contract work meaning they would not be completing the construction of the boiler for The Unknown Warrior.

We are currently in the process of looking for a new supplier who can complete the Fowler parallel boiler which will be of traditional construction with a copper firebox. It will be the first large steam locomotive boiler to be constructed in the UK since 1962.

With the added costs brought about by this situation we are launching our **Raising the Pressure!** appeal for funds dedicated to the completion of the boiler.

We are looking to raise £250,000 dedicated to the boiler construction, manufacture of the boiler cladding and installation of the boiler into the locomotive chassis.

CAN YOU HELP US RAISE THE FUNDS WE REQUIRE?

You can make a donation (which will attract 25% Gift Aid if you are a UK taxpayer) or you can sponsor a specific boiler part such as Steel Stays at £7 each up to the Superheater Header Pattern at £2,500. Go to **www.lms-patriot.org.uk/sponsorship** for the full listing.

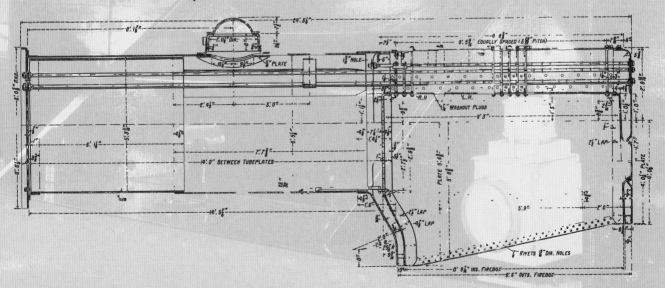

CHAPTER 5

Mix and match:

The 1948 Locomotive Exchanges

The newly nationalised railway inherited a fleet of locomotives that had been designed for, and tailored tightly to, the needs of the individual Big Four companies. However, now was the chance to see just what the finest from each company could do on the other's metals. Lineside enthusiasts never had it so good: locomotives, which normally ran on opposite ends of the country, and were suddenly on their doorsteps. Yet in so many ways it was the start of an Indian Summer for UK steam, for within a decade, dieselisation would be on the way.

During 1948, the Railway Executive sponsored a series of intensive locomotive interchange trials between the new regions of British Railways, with a view to trying out representative locomotive types of the former railway companies with standard loads.

As much as possible, identical conditions were selected, both over the routes on which the locomotives were designed primarily to work as well as others in various parts of the country. On its formation in 1948, British Railways inherited four series of modern locomotive types, one from each of the former main line companies. Although each of these series was highly standardised within a single company, hardly any features or details were common between the companies.

In pursuance of its general policy of engineering standardisation, the Railway Executive decided that it would not continue to build four varieties of locomotives for each traffic duty. Instead, as we shall see, it proposed a single series of about 12 Standard types, each of which would contain the best features of existing designs, and could be improved and developed as time went on.

Of the various methods of locomotive testing, that which gave the quickest general survey of passengers and economy was the dynamometer car,

A little bit of posing by the footplate crew as Gresley A4 No. 22 *Mallard* heads the Down 1.30pm Paddington-Penzance service through Sonning Cutting on April 26, during the 1948 Locomotive Exchanges. M W EARLEY

as famously employed on *Flying Scotsman*'s official 100mph world record run in 1934 and Mallard's 126mph all-time steam record four years later. Instruments in the dynamometer car measure drawbar pull, speed, and horsepower. The indications so given, related to the coal and water consumed, are a fair measure of the overall efficiency of the locomotive.

Fourteen types of locomotives were tried on selected routes on each of five regions, ranging as far north as Inverness and as far west as Plymouth.

The test covered the period from April to December, 1948, and the results filled 131 pages of a subsequent report.

The tests were not intended to be a contest between locomotives of similar types, which it was appreciated had been designed, for the most part, to fulfil the requirements of their particular regions. The results, therefore, did not disclose any dramatic or unexpected features, nor is it possible to declare that one type of locomotive was 'the best'.

From the outset it was realised that these indications would be of a very broad kind, as the trials were carried out under the normal operating conditions at the time of each test run and without any special preparation of the locomotives.

It was agreed that the locomotives used should be taken direct from traffic, having run between 15,000 and 20,000

Bulleid Merchant Navy Pacific No. 35017 *Belgian Marine* heads out of Wakefield Westgate in May 1948, a dynamometer car coupled behind. HM LANE/COLOUR RAIL

miles since last general repair. There was consequently some variation in mechanical conditions, particularly in the case of freight locomotives.

It was also realised that, in the existing circumstances, inequalities would be present in any variable speed testing on the track. Traffic delays and temporary speed restrictions are two such examples and, while the traffic delays tended to cancel out over a number of tests, the number and siting of temporary speed restrictions affected some locomotives more than others.

It was appreciated, however, that further testing would subsequently have to be undertaken on the Rugby and Swindon testing plants and with the mobile testing plant, when such limitations would not apply.

THE LEVEL PLAYING FIELD
The Western Region locomotives had grate and smokebox arrangements specifically designed to suit Welsh coal, and these, together with the firing technique to which the Western Region enginemen had been trained, differed from what was customary with the types of coal used on the trials.

In view of these conditions it was arranged that, on completion of the trials, additional tests should be made on the Western Region using Welsh coal.

The greatest care was taken to make the test runs as nearly comparable as possible. Every controllable factor was catered for; and unpredictable conditions such as weather, signal and permanent-way checks, and late running were all recorded, so that their influence

could be borne in mind. As the engines concerned were not all fitted with continuous blow-down, the apparatus was disabled. All three dynamometer cars used were calibrated on uniform lines at Derby before the trials began.

Coal used for lighting-up was separated from that used during actual runs; and care was taken to see that the quantity of fuel remaining in the firebox at the end of a test was about the same as at the start.

Similarly, tenders were calibrated beforehand; and then at the end of a run the water level in the boiler was brought to the same level as at the beginning of the test.

At the beginning of the report, some extremely interesting figures were given, to convey, in the briefest way,

LMS rebuilt Royal Scot 4-6-0 No. 46162 *Queen's Westminster Rifleman* passing Retford with the 1.10pm Kings Cross-Leeds and Bradford Express during the Locomotive Exchanges at 4.10pm on April 27, 1948. MICHAEL DOVE

Heading an Exeter to Paignton service, West Country No. 34009 *Lyme Regis* runs in hardcore Great Western territory along Isambard Kingdom Brunel's sea wall at Teignmouth during the 1948 Locomotive Exchanges. WS RUMBOLD

the summarised results. They show the ratios of All coal/All work for the various engines, and were derived from the grand totals for all engines of the class throughout the whole series of tests over all applicable routes.

The coal ratios were expressed in total weight (lb) divided by work done (hp/hr). Water ratios were also given to show the evaporation secured on the different locomotives; in this case the figures were: water (total weight, lb) divided by work done (hp/hr).

These results are given in the table at the end of this chapter.

The general plan of the report was to present, first, dimensions and other relevant data of the types of locomotives concerned, followed by folding tables, showing details of the test results, including coal and water consumption. Later pages gave the performance figures over selected portions of the routes (speed, horsepower, cut-off, and regulator position), notes on adhesion and slipping and draw-bar pull characteristics. Diagrams showing the oscillations encountered with the various locomotive classes were included, followed by dynamometer car records illustrating the coasting tendencies of the freight engines.

The methods of working the various locomotives were then given, followed by a five-page appraisal of the mechanical condition of the engines,

with notes on any defects that developed during the trials.

Finally, there was an appendix devoted to the additional tests carried out on the Western Region.

In contemporary issues of The Railway Magazine, Cecil J Allen published his own observations of these trials, made from the point of view of a passenger. It is interesting to examine some of the performances recorded during the trials and to see how the test data compared with Mr Allen's impressions.

TESTING TIME BEGINS

On May 14, 1948, Bulleid Merchant Navy Pacific *Belgian Marine* gave an excellent performance between Penrith and Preston with a train of 503 tons tare (525 tons full), gaining six minutes (eight mins net) over the schedule time of 86 mins for this 72.2-mile run, which includes the ascent, from the north, of the notorious Shap incline – 9½ miles in all, at gradients varying from 1-in-106 to 1-in-142.

A recorded drawbar horsepower figure of 1629 was obtained, at 49.7mph (equivalent to 1920hp on the level)

LMS Princess Coronation Pacific No 46236 *City of Bradford* in Sonning Cutting with the 1.30pm Down express on May 18, 1948. Note the dynamometer coach behind the tender. MW EARLEY

LMS Royal Scot 4-6-0 No. 46162 *Queen's Westminster Rifleman* heads through Sonning Cutting during the 1948 Locomotive Exchanges.
MW EARLEY

LNER streamlined A4 Pacific No. 60033 *Seagull* at Farnborough on June 11, 1948, during the trials.
T OWEN/COLOUR RAIL

Breaking new ground for the air-smoothed class, Bulleid West Country light Pacific No. 34006 *Bude* heads out of Aylesbury in June 1948. P HUGHES

which is even higher than Mr Allen's estimate of 1700 (assuming that he was also working on the 'equivalent' figure). The cut-off was 33%; the boiler pressure 255lb per sq in and the steam-chest pressure 2254lb per sq in. The notes on the engine-working record that a better performance seemed to be obtained when it was being worked fairly hard.

The regulator was usually Va to lA open on rising gradients, when the cut-off was normally 23-25%, the increase to 33% being required, evidently, to get the heavy train up Shap. The coal burned per mile, over the whole trip (Carlisle to Euston) averaged 50.22lb, i.e. 0.0791b per ton-mile (including engine) or 3.86lb per drawbar horsepower/hour. The corresponding water consumption was 31.80lb per drawbar horsepower/hour.

Another Bulleid engine, West Country light Pacific *Bude*, did brilliantly on runs between Marylebone and Manchester. Mr Allen noted a climb up the l-in-105 to Amersham after the earlier part of the run had been spoiled by a series of checks. The train was 360 tons (380 tons full), and speed rose from 27 to 45mph up this gradient; while later, climbing from Great Missenden to milepost 3IV2 speed only fell from 7IV2 to 60mph.

The report shows recorded drawbar horsepowers, at various points en route, as varying between 1266 and 1574 (equivalent to 1600 to l962hp) with a cut-off varying between 25 and 30%. Coal consumption was 4.07lb per dbhp/hr over the whole run, and water consumption 31.43lb per dbhp/hr.

LMS Duchess No 46236 City of Bradford enters Newton Abbott with the 1.30pm Paddington-Plymouth service on May 20, 1948, during the Locomotive Exchanges.
WJ ALCOCK

West Country light Pacific No. 34006 *Bude* backing out of Marylebone with a dynamometer car and an LMS Stanier tender during the 1948 Locomotive Exchanges. H GORDON TIDEY

WR Modified Hall 4-6-0 No. 6990 *Witherslack Hall* passes Harrow-on-the-Hill with a Manchester-Marylebone Express during the 1948 Locomotive Exchanges. CRL COLES

GWR King 4-6-0 No. 6018 *King Henry VI* leaving Wakefield on a King's Cross-Leeds & Bradford Express, its trial run, on May 10, 1948, saw it become the first King in Yorkshire. OVEREND PRESS AGENCY BRADFORD

KINGS ON THE EAST COAST MAIN LINE

The Western Region King class 4-6-0s worked under difficulties with regard to fuel when engaged on the King's Cross and Leeds trains. There was much smoke, and it was difficult to keep the fire in good condition. The engine, nevertheless, got away well, and cleared Finsbury Park very swiftly. The load was 525 tons full (495 tons tare) yet the coal consumption, in spite of the nature of the fuel was only 3.43lb per dbhp/hr (53.93lb per mile over the whole trip). Water consumption was 28.35lb per dbhp/hr.

Recorded horsepower amounted to 1480 (equivalent) at Wrenthorpe with regulator half-open and cut-off 35%. The boiler pressure then was 240lb per sq in. The report stated: "the black smoke indicated that the firing rate was too high, and this condition led, on occasions, to steam being wasted at the safety valves."

However, special additional trials were held on Western Region metals, using the Welsh coal normally supplied to Western Region engines. The average coal consumption using the Welsh coal was about 6.5% less, lb per dbhp/hr, or 9.2%, in lb per train mile.

These figures made due allowance for difference in calorific value between the two kinds of coal. With the Hall 4-6-0, the difference was far more marked, the figure being 17.7 and 19% respectively.

The Eastern Region's Gresley A4 Pacifics gave perhaps the best figures of any of the engines concerned with regard to low coal consumption per drawbar horsepower/hour.

On May 7, No. 60033 *Seagull* took a 330-ton train (345 tons full) over the mountainous route from Plymouth to Newton Abbot and thence to Paddington.

Despite a heart-breaking permanent-way restriction of 15mph at Plympton, which made it impossible to attack the 1-in-41 Hemerdon Bank in good style, *Seagull* lifted the train over the top at 18½mph.

On this run, coal consumption averaged 44.87lb per mile, or 3.19lb per dbhp/hr. Water consumption was 23.82lb per dbhp/hr. The recorded horsepower up Hemerdon Bank was 1111 (equivalent to 1598, with an equivalent drawbar pull of no fewer than 12.75 tons). Cut-off was 53% with full regulator; boiler and steam-chest pressures were 245 and 235lb per sq in respectively.

ROYAL SCOT THE SHOW STEALER

Among the most memorable revelations of the locomotive interchange trials was the capability and general excellence of the LMS Royal Scot class, as rebuilt with tapered boilers. These three-cylinder 4-6-0s weigh only 83 tons without their tenders, and yet showed that they could more than hold their own against the much larger Pacifics.

This was particularly noticeable on the runs to and from Waterloo. On June 18, 1948, No. 46154 *The Hussar*, running from Exeter Central to Waterloo, showed a drawbar horsepower of 1548 (1782 equivalent) at Crewkerne, with cut-off 30% and the regulator a quarter open. The boiler pressure was then 242lb per sq in.

Other very high powers were also recorded during this run. The coal

LMS Royal Scot 4-6-0 No. 46162 *Queen's Westminster Rifleman* at King's Cross on April 19, 1948.
THE RAILWAY MAGAZINE

LNER O1 2-8-0 No. 63789 with the GWR dynamometer car on Southern metals at Eastleigh during the Locomotive Exchanges of 1948. S TOWNROE/COLOUR RAIL

consumption was 3.46lb per dbhp/hr, the corresponding figure for water being 25.46lb. Over this run the coal used averaged 50.65lb per mile, with a load of 482 tons (515 tons full).

On the same route, the Duchess class, with the same load on June 25, showed figures of 3.00 and 25.87lb for coal and water respectively; the equivalent power recorded for Chard-Crewkerne was 1600, the cut-off being 25% and regulator first valve being full open. The boiler pressure then was 230lb per sq in.

The Merchant Navy coal and water figures were 3.49 and 30.61b per dbhp/hr. At Chard, the recorded horsepower was 1550 (equivalent), cut-off being 25%, and boiler and steam-chest pressures being 260 and 200lb per sq in respectively.

BELOW: Bulleid Merchant Navy Pacific No. 35017 *Belgian Marine* storms through Harrow & Wealdstone during the Locomotive Exchanges of 1948. THE RAILWAY MAGAZINE

WR Hall 4-6-0 No. 6990 *Witherslack Hall* enters Marylebone with the '1.56pm' during the 1948 Locomotive Exchanges. As one of the latest engines in the batch turned out of Swindon immediately after Nationalisation, No. 6990 was chosen to take part in the Locomotive Exchanges. The tender built with *Witherslack Hall*, No. 4049 and lettered British Railways, was switched with the GWR-liveried tender from No. 6997 on April 17, 1948 for the exchanges. Owing to clearance problems, the only non-GW route over which the engine could run was the Great Central Railway route from Marylebone to Manchester. It is therefore fitting that in the preservation era, it should have been restored at Loughborough, the home of today's Great Central Railway. Back in 1948, was also used in the trials between Bristol and Plymouth. H GORDON TIDEY

LNER A4 No. 22 *Mallard* at Basingstoke on June 8, 1948, during the 1948 Locomotive Exchanges.

LMS Royal Scot No. 46162 *Queen's Westminster Rifleman* at Plymouth after arrival with the 1.30pm from Paddington on May 25, 1948, with driver Frank Brooker of Camden shed at the regulator. WJ ALCOCK

Northern Eastern Railway dynamometer car No. 902502, the vehicle that recorded both *Flying Scotsman*'s 100mph run on November 30, 1934, and *Mallard*'s 126mph unbroken world record run on July 3, 1938, on display inside the Great Hall of the National Railway Museum in January 2017. Such vehicles played a vital role in the 1948 Locomotive Exchanges. ROBIN JONES

The one-time state-of-the-art equipment inside NER dynamometer car No. 902502, which was used to record historic locomotive runs. ROBIN JONES

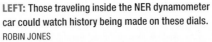

The paper reels on which the speed records were transcribed by the dynamometer car's recording equipment, as they happened. ROBIN JONES

LEFT: Those traveling inside the NER dynamometer car could watch history being made on these dials. ROBIN JONES

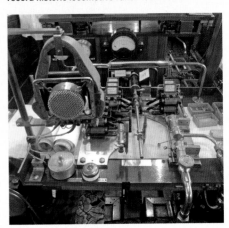

The world's fastest steam locomotive. No. 4468 *Mallard*, a veteran of the 1948 Locomotive Exchanges, on display inside the National Railway Museum at York. ROBIN JONES

Southern Railway Merchant Navy Pacific No. 35017 *Belgian Marine* leaves the turntable at Nine Elms motive power depot, newly repainted after the 1948 Locomotive Exchanges.

ED BRUTON

Region	Class	Coal consumption ratio = Coal (total wt., lb) Work done (h.p.-hr.)	Water consumption ratio = Water (total wt., lb) Work done (h.p.-hr.)
Western	4-6-0 "King"	3.57	28.58
Eastern	4-6-2 "A4"	3.06	24.32
London Midland	4-6-2 "Duchess"	3.12	27.08
London Midland	4-6-2 "6P"	3.38	25.81
Southern	4-6-2 "Merchant Navy"	3.60	30.43
Western	4-6-0 "Hall"	3.94	29.97
Eastern	4-6-0 "B1"	3.59	27.64
London Midland	4-6-0 "5"	3.54	27.99
Southern	4-6-2 "West Country"	4.11	32.64
Western	2-8-0 "2800"	3.42	26.80
Eastern	2-8-0 "O1"	3.37	25.73
London Midland	2-8-0 "8F"	3.52	27.26
	2-8-0 "Austerity"	3.77	28.75
	2-10-0 "Austerity"	3.52	28.05

WHAT HAPPENED NEXT

These are but a few examples taken from the voluminous locomotive exchange trials report. The use the Railway Executive would make of the mass of accumulated data can be summarised under two main headings:

(1) As all the locomotives demonstrated their ability to operate the selected trains to the booked timings when operating on 'foreign' routes, differing widely in character from the 'home' routes, the Railway Executive was satisfied that no limit need be placed on its proposals for standardisation by reason of suitability of particular locomotives for the routes over which they would have to work.

(2) The tests indicated many features of design worthy of consideration for the new Standard types, and the drawing offices examined closely their possible application. Examples are:

(a) Use of the largest boilers, which weight limits will allow, to give ample reserve of power for all circumstances.

(b) Use of wide fireboxes in the larger engines for highest combustion efficiency.

(c) Firebox and ashpan arrangement to give best results with varying qualities of coal.

(d) Adoption of design features to promote good riding and minimum wear and tear on the track.

The conclusions reached as a result of the trials showed that for comparable conditions and duties locomotives with wide fireboxes had a higher overall efficiency than those with narrow fireboxes, but the effect of differences in other design features reversed this in some cases.

The importance of correct firing technique in relation to the type of coal used, and the necessity for adjusting details of design, such as spacing of fire bars, to suit the type of coal used, were especially evident in connection with the higher power outputs.

There was a clear indication, too, of the advantages of high boiler output and large thermal capacity to give a reserve of power and margin for rapid recovery without an appreciable decrease in overall efficiency.

Steam temperatures were not recorded, but there were indications that an increase in the degree of superheat effected an improvement in efficiency in the case of express passenger and mixed-traffic locomotives. In the case of freight locomotives the improvement was much less marked.

The performances of the different locomotives with regard to slipping were variable, and it was recognised that further investigation was desirable. In view of the irregular

draw-bar pulls recorded in certain cases it was considered that further investigation should be made into the effect of balancing, valve setting, and other relevant factors on the smoothness of draw-bar pull.

The express passenger and mixed-traffic locomotives with the smaller diameter coupled wheels experienced no difficulty in attaining the speeds necessary to maintain schedules, and on all routes it was noted that the average power required from the locomotives was low in relation to maximum power required.

Whereas individual tests of this kind had been carried out from time to time by all the former companies, this was the first occasion on which so comprehensive a series was run. It gave the Railway Executive the opportunity of basing its locomotive design policy on known and recorded facts.

It must be appreciated, however, that the tests outlined covered only operating and performance features. These had to be supplemented for each locomotive by data on building and repair costs and on availability in daily service.

*This chapter is based on an article that appeared in The September/October 1949 issue of *The Railway Magazine*.

CHAPTER 6

TRIED
AND TESTED
designs

The first few years of British Railways saw locomotive works turning out locomotives built to classic Big Four designs, while Robert Riddles took stock of the situation after examining the results of the 1948 Locomotive Exchanges and drew up plans for new ones.

After January 1, 1948, it was more often than not a case of the UK's railways carrying on as before just as they did under the Big Four.

The paperwork to take the country's railways into state ownership had been signed, and notices to that effect had been posted at stations over the entire network.

Robert Riddles had yet to make his mark with designs for new steam locomotives for the newly created British Railways. So, to keep a rolling programme of replacement locomotive building underway to meet the needs of the network, types designed by the Big Four companies continued to be built by the respective regions while they were waiting for new classes to leap off the drawing board and on to the railway works' production lines.

British Railways built 396 steam locomotives to LNER designs, the most archaic of which was the J72 0-6-0T shunter.

Designed by William Worsdell for the North Eastern Railway as long ago as 1898, BR built 28 new examples of the class, which eventually numbered 113.

One of the most magnificent of all the BR builds of LNER designs were the Arthur H Peppercorn A1 Pacifics, a total of 49 being built between 1948-49, and his A2 Pacifics, of which 14 appeared in the first year of Nationalisation.

After Sir Nigel Gresley died suddenly in 1941, he was succeeded as Chief Mechanical Engineer by Edward Thompson, who began a much-needed programme of standardisation.

Thompson disagreed with Gresley on many aspects of locomotive design, and rebuilt or modified several of his classes, such the V2 express goods 2-6-2s, P2 Mikado 2-8-2s and even the original A1 prototype, No. 1470 *Great Northern*, a move that angered many.

His first Pacific venture was the rebuilding of Gresley's six P2 class 2-8-2s, for the sake of standardisation, despite the fact that they were regarded very much as status symbols. The rebuilds were classified as A2/2s and were the first of the Thompson rebuilds to be withdrawn.

The next batch of Thompson Pacifics were based around spare V2 boilers and were classified A2/1.

The final series of Thompson A2s were all-new engines but similar in appearance to the rebuilt locomotives and were classified by BR as A2/3s.

Thompson retired in 1946, his brief and often vilified reign having been dogged by the wartime conditions that severely restricted his scope for locomotive development. He was succeeded by Arthur H Peppercorn, then aged 57.

Born in Leominster, Herefordshire, on January 29, 1889, Peppercorn commenced his career as a Great Northern Railway apprentice in 1905, serving with the Royal Engineers during the First World War.

Many saw his appointment as reverting to the good old days of Gresley, and he pleased many at Doncaster Works by reappointing some of Gresley's former assistants.

He had been in charge for just 18 months before Nationalisation, and was left to complete many of Thompson's locomotives.

When Peppercorn took over, he halted production on a batch of 30 Thompson-designed mixed-traffic Pacifics after only half of them had been built. The remaining 15 were modified to Peppercorn's own design.

Broadly speaking, Peppercorn combined the best aspects of Gresley and Thompson designs.

The outside cylinders in the Peppercorn 'version' were restored to a more conventional position than in Thompson's A2, now that he was empowered to drop the wartime standardisation priority principle of having all the connecting rods the same length.

The end result was a far more aesthetically pleasing machine. The first of the Peppercorn A2s, No. 525

AH Peppercorn, was outshopped from Doncaster in December 1947 on the eve of Nationalisation, and named after the designer of the class. The other 14 were built in 1948.

Peppercorn's A2s reverted to having a single chimney in a period in which double chimneys were becoming widely adopted, however, the final few Peppercorn A2s reverted to a double chimney – a standard feature on his A1 Pacifics.

The A2s, of which 14 were built under him, proved to be good solid locomotives if not spectacular performers. After several years of service exclusively on the East Coast Main Line, many were sent to Scotland working both from Edinburgh and later from Glasgow's Polmadie and Corkerhill sheds. Much of their final passenger work was between Dundee or Aberdeen and Glasgow.

Peppercorn also designed and built a mixed-traffic 2-6-0, the K1, based on Thompson's two-cylinder rebuild of Gresley's K4 three-cylinder 2-6-0. A total of 70 were built between 1949-50.

Peppercorn's last and only other engines were his A1s.

Despite its troubled economic situation, despite already having more Pacifics than any of the other railways, the LNER was the only one of the Big Four to design and build new 4-6-2s in the late Forties.

Peppercorn's A1 design recalled the 6ft 8in big-wheeled express locomotive capable of long runs at high speeds.

Many of Thompson's ideas, like the divided drive, separate valve gears for each cylinder and the large free-steaming boiler with a very big firebox, formed part of the Peppercorn A1 blueprint. The production A1

The sole-surviving J72 0-6-0T, No. 69053 *Joem*, climbs up to Beck Hole on the North Yorkshire Moors Railway on May 5, 2010. More than half a century after they were first introduced, by the North Eastern Railway, British Railways built a further batch at Darlington, 20 in 1949 and eight in 1951, bringing the class total to 113. No. 99053 was built in 1951. All 113 remained in service until 1958. The design was the oldest perpetuated by the newly nationalised network. No. 69023 became the only survivor when it was purchased by Ronald Ainsworth for preservation, and moved from Holbeck shed to the Keighley & Worth Valley Railway on October 16, 1966. Three days earlier, in the middle of the night, it was driven down the East Coast Main Line through Newcastle, Durham, Darlington, York and on to the shed. It was the longest journey that the little engine would ever have made, and British Railways' staff had even made up a wooden extension to the coal rails to increase the capacity. The first two letters of Ronald's parents' names Joseph and Emmeline make up the name *Joem*.
PHILIP BENHAM/NYMR

Peppercorn A1 4-6-2 No. 60120 *Kittiwake* heads a passenger service in late June 1962. Cecil Vogel/Nigel Vogel COLLECTION/A1SLT

B1 No. 61306 *Mayflower* is one of two surviving class members. Here it is seen in action on May 3, 2014, during a North Yorkshire Moors Railway gala. It was built by the North British Locomotive Company and was outshopped on April 5, 1948, just over three months after Nationalisation. It carries LNER apple green livery with BRITISH RAILWAYS lettering on its tender sides. It received its name in preservation. PHILIP BENHAM/NYMR

Pacifics were built under Peppercorn's jurisdiction, but did not appear until BR days – hence their appearance in LNER apple green with BRITISH RAILWAYS in big lettering along the tender!

The first, No. 60114, emerged from Doncaster Works on August 6, 1948, three weeks before the last A2.

A total of 49 were built inside just 16 months, Nos. 60114-60129 and 60153-60162 at Doncaster and the rest at Darlington.

Their first 10 years saw them doing most of their work on the East Coast Main Line apart from three sent to Polmadie shed in the mid-Fifties for working some of the West Coast Main Line expresses between Glasgow and Birmingham or Crewe.

Capable of extremely hard work, the Peppercorn A1s were renowned for free steaming and very sound performances on any task. Not only that, but they managed very high mileages between overhauls.

On the east coast route, Peppercorn A1s were the only locomotives to increase steam pressure while working hard and with both injectors in use to fill the boiler with water.

Many drivers preferred the Peppercorn A1s to any other LNER class.

Another major LNER design built under BR was the Thompson L1 2-6-4T.

While the prototype, No. 9000, was built in 1945 several different manufacturers built the remaining 99 after Nationalisation.

Their 5ft 2in wheels gave them excellent power at low speed, such as that required for freight work, but

A2 Pacific No. 60532 was one of the earliest locomotives to be released for traffic under the new British Railways, outshopped by Doncaster Works on March 25, 1948. The sole survivor of the class, it is seen on static display at Barrow Hill. ROBIN JONES

this class was intended for passenger use. The speeds required for suburban passenger work wore the engines out in a remarkably short time. Axleboxes, crosshead slides and crank bearings all suffered thanks to the high speeds of suburban services.

The other class that saw members built after Nationalisation was Thompson's B1 4-6-0. It was the LNER's equivalent to the GWR's Hall and the LMS 'Black Five'; two-cylinder mixed-traffic 4-6-0s.

However, the B1s were introduced in 1942 and needed to be built on the cheap as wartime and postwar economies meant that the LNER, had to make savings where it could.

They were needed because the LNER was operating a large number of engines that were well past their economic sell-by date.

A total of 410 were built, including 136 by British Railways between 1948-52.

LNER-designed Thompson L1 2-6-4T No. 67781 being serviced beside the coaling plant at Neasden shed on March 3, 1957 nearly seven years after it was outshopped by Robert Stephenson & Hawthorn Ltd at Darlington on March 3, 1957. It was among a fleet of L1s rostered in the Fifties for the Marylebone-Princes Risborough/Aylesbury services. BEN BROOKSBANK*

BELOW: Peppercorn A1 Pacific No. 60157 *Great Eastern* leaving King's Cross Goods Yard with the 3.15pm Down goods on June 11, 1957. PETER TOWNEND/AISLT

THE SUNNY SOUTH

It was not only LNER Pacific designs that were at first perpetuated under British Railways.

Fifty of Oliver Bulleid's air-smoothed Pacifics were built after Nationalisation. There were 40 light Pacifics in the West Country and Battle of Britain classes, built between 1948-51, and 10 of the more powerful Merchant Navies, outshopped for the new Southern Region between 1948-49.

Both types were redesigned by BR in the mid-Fifties following an incident at Crewkerne station on April 24, 1953. The crank axle on the central driving wheel of Merchant Navy No. 35020 *Bibby Line* fractured while approaching the station at speed.

Although nobody was injured, all 30 Merchant Navies were withdrawn from service while the cause was ascertained. It was found that the fracture, caused by metal fatigue, was a common fault.

Classes from other regions were drafted in to deputise for the 30 while the axle was redesigned.

Making hay while the sun shone, BR decided to rebuild the Bulleid Pacifics to a more conventional design by locomotive engineer Ronald Guy Jarvis, who adopted many features from the BR Standard locomotive classes, the first of which appeared in 1951. The air-smoothed casing was removed and replaced with conventional boiler cladding, and the chain-driven valve gear was replaced with three separate sets of Walschaerts valve gear. The rebuilds were provided with a completely revised cylindrical smokebox, a new Lord Nelson-type chimney and LMS-style smoke deflectors.

Together with the lack of air-smoothed casing, these helped reduce

The first of Bulleid's Leader class, No. 36001, seen at Eastleigh in June 1949. S TOWNROE/COLOUR-RAIL

the problem of smoke and steam obscuring the driver's vision of the line ahead.

The success of the modification programme led to 60 of the light Pacifics also being modified, at Eastleigh Works between 1957-61, starting with No. 34005 *Barnstaple*.

In addition to Bulleid's famous Pacifics, British Railways also completed and steamed his even more distinctive "steam engine that thought it was a diesel" in the form of the first of his radically experimental articulated 0-6-0+0-6-0 Leader class.

The type, which had cabs at either end and the firebox in the middle, where it was fed by the fireman from a third and central cab, linked to the driving cabs at each end by a corridor, was an unorthodox attempt to extend the life of steam traction in the face of electric and diesel competition by eliminating many of the operational drawbacks associated with existing steam locomotives.

A series of initial ideas was presented to the Southern Railway management by Bulleid that incorporated double-ended running, giving the locomotive driver maximum visibility in either direction without a boiler or tender obscuring his view. The need for a turntable to turn the locomotive was therefore eliminated.

The Leader class was intended as a replacement for the ageing fleet of LSWR M7 0-4-4Ts, and was part of Bulleid's desire to modernise the steam locomotive concept based on experience gained with the Southern Railway's electric stock fleet. Design work began in 1946 and development continued after Nationalisation.

The building of five Leader locomotives was begun, although only one was completed, and it was tested on the network around Brighton. Problems with the design, indifferent reports on performance and political pressure surrounding spiralling development costs, led to all five locomotives of the class being scrapped by 1951.

THE RELUCTANT WESTERN REGION

The GWR's management was opposed to Nationalisation, and following its enforced conversion to British Railways Western Region, insisted on going it alone with regards to modernisation.

A total of 501 locomotives was built after Nationalisation to GWR designs, 341 of them being variations of the Swindon empire's trademark pannier tanks.

After the great locomotive innovator Charles Collett stood down in 1941 at the age of 70, Frederick William Hawksworth became the last Chief Mechanical Engineer of the GWR.

Hawksworth drew up plans for a direct development of the hugely successful 57XX pannier, in the form of the 9400 class.

Below the footplate, these were almost identical to the 5700s, although they were 2ft longer. However, the 94XXs had a much larger boiler, which provided more power and adhesive weight, giving greater braking capacity, wider cabs, and pannier tanks that stopped short of the smokebox, making the class instantly recognisable. The steam domes were also different.

Externally, the 94XX resembled a pannier tank version of Collett's 2251 class of 0-6-0 tender locomotives, which had appeared in 1930, sharing the same boiler and cylinders. However, the 9400s were a development of the 8750 sub-class of the 57XXs, the big difference being a taper boiler, which gave more power, and accordingly they were classified 4F by British Railways, but their greater weight, which gave them a red route restriction, was against them.

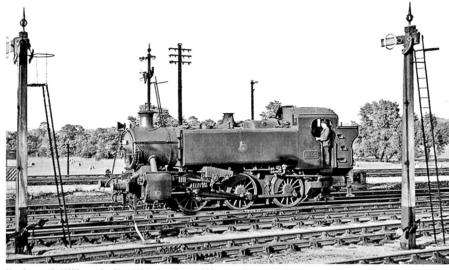

Hawksworth 15XX pannier No. 1502 shunting at Didcot on August 2, 1957. BEN BROOKSBANK*

The last 10 locomotives built by the GWR at Swindon were the first batch of 9400s, Nos. 9400-9, all of which were also equipped with superheating. After Nationalisation, a further 200 9400s were built up to 1956, but all by outside contractors, and none superheated.

Two batches, Nos. 9410-59 and 9460-89, were built between 1950-53 by Robert Stephenson & Hawthorns. The Stafford firm of W G Bagnall turned out Nos. 8400-8449 between 1949-54, and the Yorkshire Engine Company Nos. 8450-79 in 1949-52.

Subcontracted to Robert Stephenson & Hawthorns, Hudswell Clarke constructed Nos. 8480-99. Under subcontract to the Yorkshire Engine Company, Hunslet built Nos. 9490-99 in 1954-55 and Nos. 3400-9 in 1955-6. No. 8447 had a working life of just four years and nine months, being

outshopped in August 1954 and withdrawn in May 1959, the shortest of any GWR-design locomotive under British Railways.

Excellent heavy shunting locomotives, they were also used on short freight and passenger trips. Many were based at Old Oak Common for hauling empty coaching stock in and out of Paddington.

Yet, you cannot keep a classic design down, and after Nationalisation, Swindon Works turned out 41 more 57XX pannier tanks between April 1948 and December 1950. In all, a total of 863 were built since the first appeared in 1929, making them the most prolific class of the GWR, and one of the most numerous classes of British steam locomotive.

The 16XX class could trace its lineage back the 2021 class of 0-6-0STs

Built in November 1950, No. 7820 *Dinmore Manor* is seen at Bridgnorth station on the Severn Valley Railway on November 14, 2015. PETER BROSTER*

A2 Pacific No. 60532 was one of the earliest locomotives to be released for traffic under the new British Railways, outshopped by Doncaster Works on March 25, 1948. The sole survivor of the class, it is seen on static display at Barrow Hill. ROBIN JONES

this class was intended for passenger use. The speeds required for suburban passenger work wore the engines out in a remarkably short time. Axleboxes, crosshead slides and crank bearings all suffered thanks to the high speeds of suburban services.

The other class that saw members built after Nationalisation was Thompson's B1 4-6-0. It was the LNER's equivalent to the GWR's Hall and the LMS 'Black Five'; two-cylinder mixed-traffic 4-6-0s.

However, the B1s were introduced in 1942 and needed to be built on the cheap as wartime and postwar economies meant that the LNER, had to make savings where it could.

They were needed because the LNER was operating a large number of engines that were well past their economic sell-by date.

A total of 410 were built, including 136 by British Railways between 1948-52.

LNER-designed Thompson L1 2-6-4T No. 67781 being serviced beside the coaling plant at Neasden shed on March 3, 1957 nearly seven years after it was outshopped by Robert Stephenson & Hawthorn Ltd at Darlington on March 3, 1957. It was among a fleet of L1s rostered in the Fifties for the Marylebone-Princes Risborough/Aylesbury services. BEN BROOKSBANK*

BELOW: Peppercorn A1 Pacific No. 60157 *Great Eastern* leaving King's Cross Goods Yard with the 3.15pm Down goods on June 11, 1957. PETER TOWNEND/AISLT

THE SUNNY SOUTH

It was not only LNER Pacific designs that were at first perpetuated under British Railways.

Fifty of Oliver Bulleid's air-smoothed Pacifics were built after Nationalisation. There were 40 light Pacifics in the West Country and Battle of Britain classes, built between 1948-51, and 10 of the more powerful Merchant Navies, outshopped for the new Southern Region between 1948-49.

Both types were redesigned by BR in the mid-Fifties following an incident at Crewkerne station on April 24, 1953. The crank axle on the central driving wheel of Merchant Navy No. 35020 *Bibby Line* fractured while approaching the station at speed.

Although nobody was injured, all 30 Merchant Navies were withdrawn from service while the cause was ascertained. It was found that the fracture, caused by metal fatigue, was a common fault.

Classes from other regions were drafted in to deputise for the 30 while the axle was redesigned.

Making hay while the sun shone, BR decided to rebuild the Bulleid Pacifics to a more conventional design by locomotive engineer Ronald Guy Jarvis, who adopted many features from the BR Standard locomotive classes, the first of which appeared in 1951. The air-smoothed casing was removed and replaced with conventional boiler cladding, and the chain-driven valve gear was replaced with three separate sets of Walschaerts valve gear. The rebuilds were provided with a completely revised cylindrical smokebox, a new Lord Nelson-type chimney and LMS-style smoke deflectors.

Together with the lack of air-smoothed casing, these helped reduce

The first of Bulleid's Leader class, No. 36001, seen at Eastleigh in June 1949. S TOWNROE/ COLOUR-RAIL

Western Region 57XX 0-6-0PT No. 9682 at Chinnor station on August 21, 2004, during the Chinnor & Princes Risborough Railway's 10th anniversary reopening weekend. This locomotive was built in May 1949. The class was a familiar sight on many country branch lines around the time of Nationalisation. PETER SKUCE

that appeared under George Jackson Churchward in 1897. They comprised the final GWR locomotive design before Nationalisation, but did not enter traffic until afterwards. Designed by Frederick Hawksworth, 70 appeared from Swindon Works between 1949-55.

Having a large boiler but a short wheelbase, the 15XX class were the final Swindon-designed panniers of all, and the entire class of 10 appeared after Nationalisation.

They were Hawksworth's most radical design, and the all-new 12ft 10in wheelbase chassis, shorter than even the 850 class, with outside cylinders and Walschaerts valve gear, allowed the type to negotiate curves of 230ft radius.

The lack of a running plate reflected the years of austerity in which they were built. There was extensive use of welded fabrication, also one of Hawksworth's developments to combat postwar shortages. They had the same No. 10

Two Castle 4-6-0s, built after Nationalisation, survive today, in No. 7027 *Thornbury Castle*, which was outshopped in August 1949, and No. 7029 *Clun Castle*, following in May 1950. *Clun Castle* hauled the last official steam train out of Paddington (to Banbury) on June 11, 1965, and having entered preservation, became the flagship of Tyseley Locomotive Works. Following a protracted overhaul, No. 7029 was relaunched there in October 2017. It is pictured at Bristol Barrow Road on November 27, 1964. KDH ARCHIVE/TLW

Hawksworth 'Modified Hall' No. 7903 *Foremarke Hall* arrives at Toddington station on the Gloucestershire Warwickshire Railway on May 25, 2013. TONY HISGETT*

GWR 2-6-2T No. 4160 is the sole survivor of the class members built after Nationalisation. Outshopped in September 1948, it is seen at Minehead on the West Somerset Railway in June 2015. ROB HODGKINS*

boiler as the 94XXs, and their weight – they were heavier than any other 0-6-0 built by the GWR – also limited their use to red routes.

The first, No. 1500, appeared in June 1949, and the last, Nos. 1506-9, in September that year. Historians continue to question the wisdom of building the class when some of them lasted little more than a decade in British Railways' service.

Twenty more 74XX panniers were added, in two batches of 10 each in 1948 and 1950, the first batch of 30 having appeared in 1936-37. They were very similar to Collett's 64XX class of 1932, but minus the remote-control equipment for auto train working, and with a higher boiler pressure of 180psi.

At the upper end of the scale, British Railways Western Region built 30 more Castle express passenger 4-6-0s between 1948-50.

The Castles were designed by Collett and were largely based on Churchward's successful Star class of 1907. The first Castle appeared in 1923, and the first withdrawal by British Railways was in 1950.

A total of 49 new 6959 class 'Modified Hall' 4-6-0s were built at Swindon between February 1948 and November 1950, taking the fleet number up to 71.

The 'Modified Hall' is Hawksworth's development of Collett's Hall 4-6-0, and

GWR-designed pannier No. 9466, built by Robert Stephenson & Hawthorns in Newcastle in 1951, is seen heading a special to Amersham on September 7, 2013, during celebrations to mark the 150th anniversary of the Metropolitan Railway. ROBIN JONES

although they looked very similar, they were far from a simple modification of the design; indeed, nearly everything about them was new.

Ten GWR-designed Manor 4-6-0s were built by British Railways at Swindon in November and December

1950, taking the fleet number up to 30. The Manors were designed by Collett as a lighter version of the GWR Granges, giving them a wider route availability. The first 20 were built between 1938-39, and they were named after manors in the area covered by the GWR.

Swindon, 1951-built Hawksworth 16XX pannier No. 1638, at the Llangollen Railway on April 4, 2014, visiting for the spring steam gala. PETER BROSTER*

Stanier 'Black Five' No. 4767 (BR 44767) was completed at Crewe Works on the last day of the LMS, December 31, 1947, a few hours before Nationalisation. It was unique among the 842-strong class in that it featured outside Stephenson link motion in addition to experimental features including a double chimney, Timken roller bearings throughout and electric lighting. The modifications were part of a series of experiments by H G Ivatt to improve the already-excellent type. No. 4767 was renumbered 44767 by British Railways after Nationalisation, and its double chimney was replaced in 1953. It is seen heading a four-coach train at Kinchley Lane on the Great Central Railway on January 30, 2010. DUNCAN HARRIS*

Fairburn 2-6-4T No. 42611 stands at Preston on a rainy day in 1966. 70023VENUS2009*

THE INFLUENTIAL LMS

As we shall see, LMS locomotive design and practice heavily influenced what lay around the corner after Nationalisation, largely because of the presence of the company's former vice-president, Robert Riddles.

In the meantime, 640 LMS-designed locomotives were built under British Railways at various BR works, not just at the ex-LMS works at Crewe, Derby and Horwich.

A hundred of Stanier's 'Black Fives' were built between 1948-51, numbered 44658-757, taking the class total to 842, one of the biggest UK steam classes of all in numerical terms.

Introduced by William Stanier in 1934, the 'Black Fives' were a mixed-traffic locomotive, one that was all but universally adaptable and hugely popular among crews. They were influenced by Collett's Halls – Stanier had joined the LMS from the GWR – but

had a greater route availability. Class members survived in service until the last day of steam on the British Railways main line in 1968.

The Ivatt 4MT 2-6-0 was primarily designed for medium-freight work but was also widely used on secondary passenger services. Three of them were built before Nationalisation, and 159 afterwards, the last one in 1952.

British Railways used them extensively across the London Midland Region, also becoming the dominant type on the Midland & Great Northern Joint Railway.

Also designed by H G Ivatt was the 2MT 2-6-2T, a small Class 2 locomotive a design that was intended to replace ageing tank engines across the system. It featured labour-saving devices such as rocking grates and self-emptying ashpans. The design was based on the Stanier 2-6-2T which was, in turn, based on the Fowler 2-6-2T.

The last of William Stanier's Princess Coronation Pacifics, No. 46257 *City of Salford*, was built by British Railways and is carrying the early express passenger blue livery in this contemporary postcard. ROBIN JONES COLLECTION

Ivatt 4MT 2-6-0 No. 43106, the sole survivor of a class of 162, with a driving course special at Bewdley on the Severn Valley Railway on February 28, 2015. The type acquired the nickname 'Flying Pig'. ROBIN JONES

LMS Ivatt 2MT 2-6-2T No. 41287 at Guildford in May 1963. HUGH LLEWELYN*

A total of 130 were built, all but 10 after Nationalisation at Crewe and Derby. A tender version, the Ivatt 2MT 2-6-0, was also produced. A total of 128 were built between 1946 and 1953, all but 20 by LMS. Following attention to draughting problems by both Derby and Swindon, the class quickly became a success.

By far the biggest LMS class to continue in production after Nationalisation was Charles Fairburn's 2-6-4T. Fairburn was made Acting Chief Mechanical Engineer of the LMS when Stanier was called away on war work in 1942 at the Ministry of Production

and became CME in 1944 on Stanier's retirement.

In 1945 he introduced a modified version of the LMS Stanier 2-6-4T with a shortened wheelbase, to allow curves of five chains to be negotiated.

A total of 277 of his 2-6-4Ts were built, of which 147 were constructed by British Railways, at Derby and Brighton works. Fairburn died of a heart attack aged 58 on October 12, 1945, and was succeeded by H G Ivatt.

One of the more unusual LMS locomotives to be built after Nationalisation was a Kitson 0-4-0ST light shunter, which was similar in

appearance to industrial types. Five were ordered in 1932 to Stanier's specifications, and five more were built by British Railways at Horwich Works in 1955. This second batch had shorter saddle tanks with extra space given to longer coal bunkers instead. Some were used on the Cromford & High Peak Railway in the Peak District.

Finally, British Railways built the last example of Stanier's Duchess Pacifics in No. 46257 *City of Salford*, which emerged from Crewe Works on May 22, 1948. As one of the altered examples of the class, it was built without the streamlined casings of the original.

LMS Kitson 0-4-0ST No. 47001 at Barrow Hill shed near Chesterfield on August 23, 1963. BEN BROOKSBANK*TSON

CHAPTER 7

Setting new
Standards

Three years after Nationalisation, British Railways was no longer content to merely keep on building new locomotives to tried-and-tested Big Four designs. In 1951, the first of its own Standard classes appeared, and over the next nine years, 12 Standard types totalling 999 locomotives were built. However, while by and large they were excellent machines, through no fault of their own the Standards marked the final curtain falling on the UK steam age.

As Mechanical Engineer with the newly formed Railway Executive, Robert Riddles was in no doubt that the long-term future of Britain's railways would lay with electric traction. However, those times were yet to come, and in the dark days of postwar austerity, seemed light years away.

Riddles openly argued the case for steam, claiming that it was cheaper than the alternatives then on offer. He pointed out that the new diesels were not the equal of a Class 8 Pacific.

In his presidential address to the Institution of Locomotive Engineers in November 1950, he compared capital costs of new-build.

He said that a Class 5 steam locomotive would cost £16,000, compared with £78,100 for a 1600hp diesel, £138,700 for a gas turbine locomotive, or £37,400 for an electric locomotive. He calculated the costs per drawbar horse power as £13 6s (steam), £65 (diesel), £69 7s (turbine) and £17 13s (electric).

To serve the needs of the nationalised rail network, Riddles designed and built a set of 12 standard locomotive designs.

Coming off the drawing board in the wake of the Locomotive Exchanges of 1948, the BR Standards, as they came to be known, officially incorporated the best practices of all of the Big Four railway companies. Five of the 12 classes were visibly based on LMS design and practice; the Standard 5 4-6-0 (a direct successor to the hugely successful LMS 'Black Five'), the Standard 4 2-6-0 and 2-6-4 tank engine (both based on the LMS 2-6-4T), and the Class 2 2-6-0 and 2-6-2T.

Characteristic features were taper boilers, high running plates, two cylinders and streamlined cabs, with the emphasis almost exclusively on two-cylinder designs.

Three Pacific classes, the 9F 2-10-0, the Class 4 4-6-0 and the Class 3 2-6-0 and 2-6-2T were new designs.

Drawing on his experience with building the WD Austerities, Riddles designed his Standards for simplicity, ease of maintenance – where individual components were easier to access – and the ability to use cheap poor-quality coal. In so many ways, Riddles continued LMS Chief Mechanical Engineer H G Ivatt's steam locomotive policy, which was mainly directed towards the reduction of maintenance costs, as exemplified by the adoption of self-cleaning smokeboxes and rocking grates. The Big Four had placed great emphasis on big glamour locomotives that would inspire the public imagination. Under British Railways, however, in an age of thrift, functionality was the prime requirement. Postwar Britain was a very different place to what it had been in the Thirties, a time regarded by many as the golden age of steam.

GWR engineer, George Jackson Churchward, would have been well pleased by the fact that all of Riddles' 12 classes had the same range of standard parts and detail fittings. Standardisation of parts among classes contributed enormously to the huge success of the GWR steam fleet in the 20th century.

Riddles' Standards were the ultimate development of the steam locomotive in Britain, eventually bringing the proud world-shaping history that had begun with Richard Trevithick's first experiments with railway locomotives at Coalbrookdale in 1802 and on the Penydarren Tramroad near Merthyr Tydfil in 1804, to a close.

No. 70000 *Britannia* heading the London Victoria to Exeter St David's leg of the Railway Touring Company's 'Great Britain VIII' railtour passes Padworth level crossing at Aldermaston on April 28, 2015. JUSTIN FOULGER*

FORGING AHEAD
BRITISH RAILWAYS   BRITISH RAILWAYS
THE FIRST BRITISH RAILWAYS STANDARD EXPRESS LOCOMOTIVE

A contemporary British Railways' poster advertising the first of a new breed of steam locomotives.

A very rare photograph of No. 70000 running on the West Coast Main Line north of Crewe in January 1951, in black and minus its nameplates, before its naming ceremony by Minister for Transport Alfred Barnes at Marylebone station on January 30, 1951. It had emerged from Crewe Works on January 2 that year, it was painted in unlined black, carrying the number 70000 on the cabsides and smokebox, and with a plain 7 above the number on the cabside. It ran in the black livery for several days of test runs, including at least one trip over Shap. After the naming, *Britannia* ran in Brunswick Green livery for the rest of its career for British Railways and for all but a brief period in preservation in 2010, when it reverted to black. No. 70000 was chosen to haul the funeral train of King George VI from King's Lynn to London following the king's death in February 1952, and has its cab roof painted white as was the custom with Royal Train locomotives. COLOUR-RAIL

Britannia was sold to Pete Waterman in 2000 for overhaul at Crewe Works. The project was completed after the locomotive was transferred to Jeremy Hosking's Royal Scot Locomotive and General Trust, and was returned to main line operating condition in 2011, initially out-shopped in its prototype black British Railways' livery. After a running-in period, in 2012 the locomotive was repainted in BR Brunswick green, but with an early BR crest. On January 24, 2012, with its cab roof again painted white, No. 70000 hauled the Royal Train with Prince Charles on board to Wakefield Kirkgate, where he alighted to rededicate the locomotive following the completion of its latest overhaul. ROBIN JONES

THE FIRST OF THE NEW BREED

The first Standard to appear was Class 7 two-cylindered Pacific No. 70000 *Britannia*, Riddles' response to the Railway Executive's demand for a new express passenger 4-6-2.

It was designed at Derby and outshopped by Crewe Works in 1951, the year of the Festival of Britain, and officially named by Transport Minister Alfred Barnes on January 30.

The choice of the name *Britannia* for the first of the new Pacifics reflected Riddles' affection for the LNWR where he began his railway career. It meant renaming the LMS Jubilee that already carried the name. Further members of the class were named after great Britons, but the name Britannia was also used to refer to the rest of the 55-strong class, which was built at Crewe between 1951-54.

Their basic design owed much to LMS building practices, but in keeping with the necessity to follow best practice in creating standardised steam locomotives, they utilised a variation of both boiler and trailing wheel of the Southern Railway Merchant Navy 4-6-2s, while weight was kept within the margins laid down by the light Pacifics, all of which were designed by Oliver

Bulleid. The lighter weight increased the route availability of a Pacific-type locomotive on the British Railways' network

They had 6ft 2in driving wheels, following Bulleid's Pacifics and Peppercorn's LNER A2s, which had proved that this was no obstacle to high-speed performance. The wheelsize facilitated sustained fast running with heavy passenger trains, yet were small enough to for use on freight workings.

The Britannias, which made a name for themselves on Great Eastern lines, and indeed revolutionised these routes for a decade, were more often than not warmly welcomed by their crews, with those regularly operating the locomotives giving them favourable reports as regards performance. However, trials in some areas of the British Railways' network returned negative feedback, primarily owing to indifferent operation of the locomotive, with its effects on adhering to timetables.

Some went to the Western Region to supplement the Castles, but that region generally hated them. The criticism was primarily out of preference for GWR-designed locomotive stock among Western Region staff. Nationalisation may have brought the Big Four together in one big melting pot, but old loyalties died hard or did not die at all.

One major criticism of the Western Region was that the class was left-hand drive in contrast to right-hand drive. For this reason, the Western Region locomotive depots at Old Oak Common and Plymouth Laira declared the class surplus to requirements, but across the border in Wales, crews at Cardiff Canton shed liked them, and produced good results with them on passenger services.

Two of the Britannias, for internal BR political reasons, went to the Southern Region and worked the 'Golden Arrow' to Dover.

The LMR had a few spread around the region, and a handful went to Scotland. On the LMR, they became the last working British Pacifics.

If steam had lasted another 40 years, hundreds of Britannias may have been produced and maybe they would have ultimately displaced Castles, Bulleid light Pacifics, Royal Scots and LNER V2s, reducing operating and maintenance costs, but with modernisation waiting in the wings, it was never going to happen. As it was, the Britannia Pacifics had ridiculously short lives on the front-line services they were designed for.

RIGHT: Britannia Pacific No. 70005 *John Milton*, which was built in April 1951, stands at Birmingham New Street with the 10.05am express from Glasgow Central on April 16, 1955, This locomotive was withdrawn in July 1967. BEN BROOKSBANK*

No. 70000 *Britannia* was initially based at Stratford shed (30A) in order to work East Anglian expresses to Norwich and Great Yarmouth, but was also particularly associated with the 'Hook Continental' boat train to Harwich. It was later allocated to Norwich Thorpe, March, Willesden, Crewe North, Crewe South and was withdrawn from Newton Heath on May 28, 1966, after only 15 years' service. It was stored because of its historic significance, being earmarked for the National Collection but sister No. 70013 *Oliver Cromwell* was chosen instead. *Britannia* escaped the cutter's torch after being bought by enthusiasts under the banner of the Britannia Locomotive Company Ltd. It was moved to the Severn Valley Railway in April 1971 for its restoration to be completed, and is seen opposite another Riddles Standard, 4MT 2-6-4T No. 80079, at Bridgnorth. *Britannia* steamed again for the first time in 12 years in May, 1978 and was renamed on the 20th of that month by none other than Riddles himself! No. 70000 was too heavy for regular use on the Severn Valley, and moved to the Nene Valley Railway, where it was based from 1980-2000, in-between which it returned to the main line on July 27, 1991, hauling charters. SVR ARCHIVES

THE CLAN PACIFICS

The Britannia Pacifics were followed by 10 smaller-boilered Standard 6 or Clan Pacifics in 1951-52.

At the time, increased loads over secondary routes were frequently being double-headed by regional Class 5 types, and a more powerful, more economic locomotive with similar route availability was required.

Riddles and his team decided to use a modified Class 7 chassis, fitted with a smaller boiler, creating a mixed-traffic two-cylinder Class 6, increasing its route availability in its intended area of operations, the west of Scotland, being allocated to Carlisle Kingmoor and Glasgow Polmadie. The choice of the Pacific wheel arrangement was dictated by the requirement for a wide firebox,

which could produce steam from poorer coal. The additional build and maintenance cost was offset against the savings on coal, and it was planned to build 117 in all.

Designed at the Derby Works drawing offices, the new class was constructed at Crewe.

The initial order was for 25 locomotives, but such was the immediacy of demand regarding what was a smaller version of the Britannias that a batch of 10 was rushed through construction before teething problems had been ironed out at British Railways' Rugby testing station.

The first Standard Class 6MT was turned out in 1952 at a cost of £20,426 and carried the number 72000. The initial batch, numbered 72000-72009,

were allocated to the Scottish Region, and named after Scottish clans, No. 72000 becoming *Clan Buchanan*.

Tests carried out by the Scottish Regional Executive reported that the Clan was a fast and economical engine, light on both coal and water, able to run to, and make up time, with "the steaming capacity of the boiler a revelation".

Locomotive crews, especially those at Carlisle Kingmoor shed, thought the Clans were fine machines. They operated daily over some of BR's most testing routes, encompassing Beattock, Shap, Settle and Carlisle, and the tortuous 'Port Road' to Stranraer.

An impressive run timed over the Settle and Carlisle was made by No. 72005 *Clan MacGregor* on the 12-coach

'Thames-Clyde' relief on the Settle and Carlisle line.

A total of 141.5mins from Carlisle and over the Pennines to Leeds route, including temporary speed restrictions, gave an average speed of 45mph: today's quickest schedule, using modern diesel units is 149mins.

However, trials in other areas of the national network returned negative feedback, a common complaint being that difficulty in steaming the locomotive made it hard to adhere to timetables. Reports exist that suggest a degree of the disappointment with these locomotives was attributable to their being allocated to Class 7 work when they were in reality only a Class 6; a problem ascribed to their very similar appearance to the BR Standard Class 7.

No more Clans were constructed owing to the steel shortages of the 1950s, and after the publication of the 1955 Modernisation Plan, all orders for new express passenger locomotives were cancelled, including another 91 Britannias. A fleet of 15 Clans had been pencilled in for the Southern Region, but it was not to be. Had they been built, they would have incorporated some improvements.

The class was ultimately deemed a failure by British Railways, and the last Clan was withdrawn in 1966. They are widely considered to have been the least-successful Standard design.

LEFT: BR Standard 6 Pacific No. 72004 *Clan MacDonald* at Shap Wells near Shap summit on July 3, 1954. SSLC/NEVILLE STEAM COLLECTION

BELOW: A rare appearance south of the border saw BR Clan Pacific No. 72005 *Clan MacGregor* alongside Chester 3A signalbox at Chester General with a freight working on August 29, 1964. BEN BROOKSBANK*

Caprotti valve gear-fitted BR Standard 5MT No. 73142 waits at St Pancras Platform 3 with the 10.50am express to Leicester on June 13, 1957. BEN BROOKSBANK

BELOW: BR Standard 5MT 4-6-0 No. 73156 undergoing a test run at Loughborough on the Great Central Railway on September 8, 2017, following a lengthy restoration from Barry scrapyard condition. This locomotive was one of nine examples built at Doncaster, and was outshopped in December 1956 to be allocated to Neasden depot (34E) at the London end of the Great Central main line. Withdrawn by BR in November 1967, it spent nearly 19 years in Barry scrapyard before it was bought in 1985 by the North West Locomotive Action Group which formed the Bolton Steam Locomotive Company Ltd to restore it. The restoration began at Bury on the East Lancashire Railway and was completed at Loughborough on the modern-day Great Central. ANDREW MORLEY

THE STANDARD 5MT: AN IMPROVEMENT ON THE 'BLACK FIVES'

William Stanier's LMS 'Black Five' 4-6-0, an all-purpose mixed-traffic type, proved so successful that 842 were built, making them one of the biggest classes in British railway history.

Riddles' successor to the 'Black Five', the Standard 5MT 4-6-0, had 6ft 2in, rather than 6ft driving wheels, and could reach 100mph if steamed properly. The locomotive featured a BR standard boiler very similar in dimensions to the Stanier Type 3B fitted to the 'Black Fives', but was made from manganese

Standard 5MT No. 73129, which was also restored from Barry scrapyard condition, is the only surviving example of the 30 members of the class that were built with Caprotti value gear. It is seen hauling a special at its Midland Railway-Butterley home on July 26, 2009. ROBIN JONES

instead of nickel steel.

Again, the Standard design incorporated features designed to make disposal easier: a self-cleaning smokebox and a rocking grate removed the necessity for crews to undertake dirty and strenuous duties at the end of a long shift. The most obvious visible sign that ease of maintenance was a priority, was the high running plate, well clear of the driving wheels, a feature of all but the smallest of the Standard range.

Riddles envisaged his design to be more economical and serviceable replacements for the Bulleid Pacifics. Design was carried out at Doncaster Works but most of the construction was done at Derby. Other differences between a Standard 5MT and a 'Black Five' were a standard cab with external pipework and the regulator gland on the driver's side of the boiler below the dome.

The first of 172 5MTs, No. 73000, was outshopped from Derby in April 1951 and 30 were in service by January 1952. The last of 172 appeared from Derby in June 1957.

The class hauled much of the traffic on the last express lines for steam in the mid- and late-1960s: Edinburgh-Aberdeen, London- Southampton-Bournemouth-Weymouth and local express traffic in the North and Midlands around Sheffield and Leeds.

They were also used on the locals between Liverpool, Manchester and Blackpool, some of which were steam hauled to the last day of steam in 1968.

Thirty 5MTs, Nos. 73125 to 73154, were built with Caprotti valve gear and poppet valves.

Lined Brunswick green-liveried BR Standard 4-6-0 No. 75029 *The Green Knight* is seen emerging light engine from Grosmont Tunnel on the North Yorkshire Moors Railway. It emerged from Swindon Works in May 1967 and was withdrawn in August 1967 having had a service life of just 13 years. However, it was not sent to a scrapyard but bought out of service by the late wildlife artist David Shepherd, who named it and set up the East Somerset Railway on a truncated section of the GWR Cheddar Valley line so it could run both it and BR Standard 9F No. 92223 *Black Prince*, which he also bought straight from BR. ROBIN JONES

After 12 years under overhaul at the heritage line's Churston Works, BR Standard 4-6-0 No. 75014, which acquired the name *Braveheart* in preservation, returned to service in late 2016 and is seen climbing past Waterside on the Dartmouth Steam Railway on December 11.
MARK WILKINS

THE 4MT 4-6-0:
THE 'SUPER MANORS'

As well as the Standard 5MT 4-6-0, Riddles designed 4MT classes; a 4-6-0 and a 2-6-4T.

Design work was done at Brighton by Riddles with help from Swindon, Derby and Doncaster.

Construction of the 4-6-0 was at Swindon Works. These engines were the size of the GWR Manor 4-6-0s, and they were essentially a tender version of Riddles' BR Standard 4 2-6-4T, but unlike the Manors they were built to the universal loading gauge.

Therefore they had much greater route availability (on routes where weight restrictions prohibited Class 5s) than either the Manor or the Standard 5MT.

Eighty of these engines were built, all at Swindon; many for the Western Region, but some went to the LMR, and the later batches to the SR, with bigger tenders because of the lack of water troughs.

Some were given double chimneys, which improved performance and economy, but this addition was never extended to the whole class.

The 4-6-0s and 2-6-4Ts used the same running gear and substantially the same firebox, smokebox and boiler, although the boiler barrel was increased in length by 9in on the tender engines.

The leading bogie was identical to the Standard 5MT 4-6-0, but the driving wheels were 5ft 8in as opposed to 6ft 2in.

Critics said that there was too small a difference between many of the Standard classes, and wondered if all of them were really necessary.

BR Standard 4MT 4-6-0 No. 75027 at Sheffield Park on the Bluebell Railway. BARRY LEWIS*

No. 75000 became the first of Riddles' Standard 4MT 4-6-0s when it emerged from Swindon Works, where all 80 members of the class were built, in May 1951. The last one appeared in May 1957.
BRITISH RAIL

LMS Fairburn 2-6-4T No. 42085 at the Lakeside & Haverthwaite Railway, on March 28, 2010. A total of 277 of these, designed by Charles Fairburn for the LMS, were built between 1945-51. This design was based on the earlier LMS Stanier 2-6-4T, which in turn was derived from Henry Fowler's LMS Fowler 2-6-4T. It was also the basis for the BR Standard 4MT tank. DAN DAVISION*

BR Standard 4MT 2-6-4T No. 80135 heads a North Yorkshire Moors Railway passenger train on June 18, 2012. ROBIN JONES

THE STANDARD 4MT 2-6-4T: EVOLVING ANOTHER LMS DESIGN

At Nationalisation, the London Midland Region inherited a number of LMS tank engines and the Western Region had many GWR large prairie 2-6-2T types.

These locomotives were particularly suited to commuter and secondary services. However, in certain areas particularly in Scotland and the Southern Region, the situation was not so good with large numbers of pre-Grouping types soldiering on.

Designed at Brighton, these were a tank version of the BR Standard 4MT 4-6-0. A total of 155 were built between 1951-56, mostly in Brighton with small batches in Derby and Doncaster. They were, in many respects, an updated version of the LMS Fairburn 4P 2-6-4Ts but with higher boiler pressure and smaller cylinders to fit within the BR loading gauge.

They were shared between the Southern Region, LMR and Scottish Region, with a few on the North Eastern Region. The Western Region did not need them as it had ample GWR 2-6-2Ts.

After Nationalisation, the Southern Region built 41 LMS Fairburn 2-6-4Ts at Brighton Works for its own use, replacing much older tank engines. However, once the new Standard 2-6-4Ts came on stream, these replaced the LMS-designed ones on the SR.

They became particularly associated with the London, Tilbury & Southend line, until it was electrified in 1962, and with Glasgow's suburban services.

The Standard 4MT tanks were more handsome in appearance than their LMS predecessors, and were well liked by their crews for their comfortable cabs, free running, good steaming and economical operation. They performed their duties well but were very quickly replaced by more modern traction on the kind of duties they were designed for. An order for further engines was cancelled as it was becoming clear they would not be needed because of dieselisation and electrification.

RIGHT: Numerically the first of the class, No. 80000 was the first BR Standard 4MT 2-6-4T to be built at Derby, but the first overall to be built was No. 80010, at Brighton Works. BRITISH RAIL

A Tunbridge-Brighton service enters Tunbridge Wells West station behind BR Standard 4MT 2-6-4T No. 80150 on June 18, 1961. This locomotive was one of the last to leave Barry scrapyard and is currently at the Mid Hants Railway awaiting restoration. BEN BROOKSBANK*

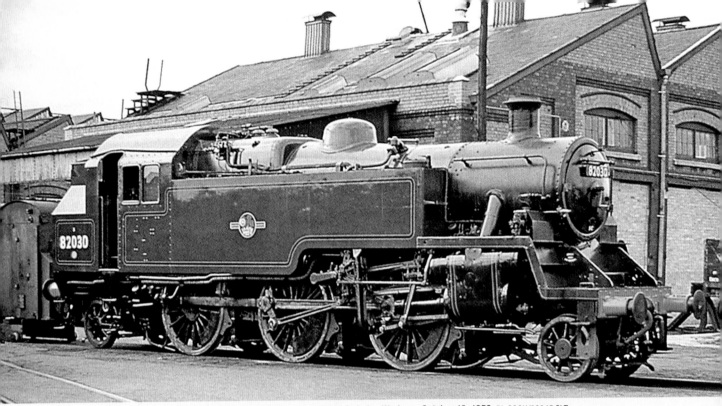

In Brunswick green livery, BR Standard 3MT 2-6-2T No. 82030 stands outside Swindon Works on October 18, 1959. RL COOK/82045 SLT

THE BR STANDARD 3MT TANK: A LMS/GWR HYBRID

H G Ivatt had initiated a standardisation programme for the LMS, which envisaged six types, but Riddles planned another three and his BR Standard 3MT 2-6-2Ts were one of the additional ones.

The Class 3 2-6-2T was a hybrid design, the chassis being closely based on, and sharing several parts, with the LMS Ivatt Class 4, and having a boiler derived from a GWR No. 2 boiler as fitted to the GWR large prairie 2-6-2T and 56XX 0-6-2T.

The design and construction took place at the ex-GWR Swindon Works, along with the 2-6-0 tender engine

version of the class, the 77XX. Although the boiler shared flanged plates with the GWR No.2 boiler, the barrel was shortened by 5 13/16in and a dome was added.

In common with several other Riddles' Standard classes, the chassis design used many LMS-designed components including brake hanger brackets, flexible stretcher brackets and reversing shaft brackets. The LMS 'roots' of many of the Standard classes showed Riddles' very strong influence.

The motion brackets were derived from the design of those fitted to the LMS Ivatt Class 2 2-6-0 and LMS Ivatt

Class 2 2-6-2T. A total of 45 Standard 3 tanks were built between April 1952 and August 1955. From new, they were based on the Western, Southern, North Eastern and London Midland regions.

Excellent locomotives, with a design lifespan to 40 years, time was not on their side. In 1955, British Railways published its Modernisation Plan calling for the eradication of steam.

Accordingly, the class had a short life as most of the work that they had been built for soon disappeared with the branch lines; the closure of which had begun several years before Beeching, and the introduction of diesel multiple units on shorter routes.

The shortest-lived example was No. 82043, which was only eight years and eight months old at withdrawal, while the longest-lived was No. 82019, withdrawn two months before its 15th birthday.

The last two Standard 3 tanks in service were Nos. 82019 and 82029 at Nine Elms but four more survived until after the end of steam. Nos. 82000, 82003, 82031 and 82034 were transferred from North Wales at the end of 1966 to Patricroft shed in Manchester for use on local suburban trains. They were not really required, however, but lingered there until the shed's closure in 1968.

One of these four had run very few miles since its final overhaul, and enquiries were made about saving it, but the price being asked (£1500, a fortune in those days) was too high and despite the establishment of a handful of standard gauge heritage lines by that date, the four went for scrap at Cashmores in Newport, South Wales, being broken up as late as October 1968.

BR Standard 3MT 2-6-2T No. 82026 on station pilot duty at Waterloo in 1965. CHRIS WARD*

Riddles' Standard 3MT2-6-0 No.77012 in its last days at York shed, July 1967. HUGH LLEWELLYN

STANDARD 3MT 2-6-0: A POINTLESS PROJECT?

Like the 3MT 2-6-2, the tender version was also mainly designed at Swindon, although some details were designed at Brighton, Derby and Doncaster.

It was basically another a hybrid design, the chassis being closely based on and sharing a number of parts with the LMS Ivatt Class 4, and having a boiler derived from a GWR No. 2 boiler as fitted to the GWR large prairie 2-6-2Ts and 5600 Class 0-6-2Ts. They were built at Swindon between February and September 1954.

It was another type that had not been identified by H G Ivatt in his pre-Nationalisation standardisation plan for the LMS, but drawn up by Riddles afterwards. Indeed the need for them was questionable.

Only 20 were built, Nos. 77000–77019, all at Swindon and they were allocated to the North Eastern and Scottish regions. The building of such a small class makes a nonsense of the concept of standardisation but perhaps many more would have been built if they had not appeared literally the year before BR decided on large-scale dieselisation.

Nevertheless the class was at least notable for being the last class of steam locomotive on BR to remain complete before withdrawals began in 1965, the last one going out of traffic in 1967.

Riddles' Standard 3MT 2-6-0 No. 77001 after being outshopped from Swindon. BRITISH RAILWAYS

BR Standard 4MT 2-6-0s on July 27, 1963: No. 76065 leaving Salisbury with a service for Pokesdown while passing No. 76064, which is heading a train for Waterloo. BEN BROOKSBANK*

THE STANDARD 4MT 2-6-0: THE NEW FREIGHT MOGUL

This class was designed at Doncaster, which was also responsible for building 25 of the 115-strong class. The remaining 90 were split between Horwich and Derby. They were allocated to every BR region except the Western.

The design was almost identical to the Ivatt Class 4 2-6-0, as built by British Railways, which the LMS had introduced as a double-chimney design in 1947.

BR took that design modifying parts and fittings to comply with BR standard practice

With its 5ft 3in diameter driving wheels, this BR design was clearly oriented towards freight working. An axle loading of only 16 long tons 15 cwt

Restored BR Standard 4MT 2-6-0 No. 76084 hauling the North Norfolk Railway's four-coach suburban set towards Weybourne. NNR

meant its route availability was virtually unrestricted.

The last in the series, No. 76114, was also the final steam engine to be constructed at 'The Plant' (as Doncaster Works was known). The design was basically an updated version of the LMS Ivatt 4MT mogul, and was primarily intended for freight duties.

Although a Standard design, the 4MT 2-6-0 did not have the same design of wheels as the Swindon-built 3MT 2-6-0 and 2-6-2T, which also had 5ft 3in driving wheels, although all three locomotive classes share the same cylinder casting.

Most of the London Midland Region's batch of 15 spent their working lives in Lancashire but a few were allocated to the Nottingham area.

At first the North Eastern Region scattered its allocation of 13 to various areas but eventually they were all concentrated on the trans-Pennine Stainmore route where their light axle loading was necessary.

Thirty-five of the class were allocated to the Scottish Region, and used on the Waverley Route between Carlisle and Hawick and the 'Port Road' from Dumfries to Stranraer. Others were allocated to Ayrshire and around Glasgow, and to Aberdeen and Thornton Junction.

However, it was never ideal operating practice to spread a class out so thinly across such a wide area.

The Southern originally had 37 of the new moguls, far more sensibly concentrated around Eastleigh, Southampton and Bournemouth. The SR engines included 17, which were equipped with the larger BR1B tenders, and had a higher axle load than the locomotives.

LEFT: BR Standard 4MT 2-6-0 No. 76017 at Ropley on the Mid Hants Railway in the early 1980s. BARRY LEWIS*

BR Standard 2MT 2-6-0 No. 78019 heads towards Kinchley Lane on a snowbound January 26, 2013, during the Great Central Railway's winter steam gala. ROBIN JONES

RIDDLES' 2MT 2-6-0: SMALLEST OF THE STANDARD TENDER ENGINES

Designed at Derby in 1953, the smallest of the tender engines were a very slightly modified version of H G Ivatt's LMS 2MT mogul that appeared in 1946, with a reduced cab to enable it to fit into a universal loading gauge and with their external design tidied up, giving better route availability.

Darlington Works was responsible for building the entire fleet of 65 engines and for a time construction of the LMS and BR designs overlapped.

The last, No. 78064, was completed in 1956 but the class remained intact for just seven years. The provision of this class may not appear to have been necessary, but BR had inherited many

ancient 0-6-0s and tank engines and the 2MTs were a big improvement on these.

Like the LMS counterpart, the Standard mogul was arranged for a low axle loading of just 13.75 long tons, allowing it to operate on most lightly laid routes and secondary lines.

Among crews the 2MT 2-6-0 gained a reputation for being very sure-footed while others maintained that the engines did not steam well and had draughty and dirty footplates.

In some areas, the Standard 2MTs were preferred for passenger workings while the near-identical LMS ones shunted and worked goods trains.

A double-headed return Cambrian Coast holiday express at Barmouth in 1962. The Pwllheli to Birmingham (Snow Hill) service is head by BR Standard 2MT 2-6-0 No. 78007 piloting BR Standard 3MT 2-6-2T No. 82033.

BR Standard Class 8P 4-6-2 No. 71000 *Duke of Gloucester* in BR lined green livery with 1956 emblem blasting through Bedminster on the Bristol Temple Meads to Paignton 'Torbay Express' on July 18, 2010. HUGH LLEWELLYN*

BELOW: *Duke of Gloucester* on static display at Tyseley Locomotive Works open day on November 25, 2015. This locomotive and BR Standard 5MT No. 73129 are the only engines with Caprotti gear left in Britain. ROBIN JONES

THE LONE 8P PACIFIC: *DUKE OF GLOUCESTER*

An element of mystery has always surrounded the building of just one BR Standard 8P Pacific, No. 71000 *Duke of Gloucester*.

Riddles wanted to build a series of new 8P Pacifics but the British Railway Board refused to authorise it. It has been suggested that the LMR was short

of an 8P after LMS Princess Royal 4-6-0 No. 46202 *Princess Anne* was destroyed in the Harrow & Wealdstone crash of 1952, and Riddles managed to obtain permission to build a prototype that would effectively replace the missing engine in the fleet.

Although designed at Derby in 1953 and built at Crewe the following year, the extent of Riddles' involvement in it has been questioned.

John Frederick (Freddie) Harrison was born in Settle, and educated at Malvern Wells and Wellington College. He joined the GNR at Doncaster in 1921 and in 1923 became a pupil of Nigel Gresley. After various jobs on the GC section in the North West, in 1937 he became an assistant to the works manager at Doncaster under Edward Thompson, but quickly moved back to Gorton as locomotive works manager in 1938. While Harrison was at Gorton, Gresley showed an interest in Caprotti valve gear. Thompson promoted Harrison to be mechanical engineer of the GC section and in 1945 he was transferred to Cowlairs as mechanical engineer (Scotland). Peppercorn made him assistant CME of the LNER in 1947.

On Nationalisation he became mechanical and electrical engineer, Doncaster, for the Eastern and North Eastern regions and in July 1951 he was

BR Standard 2MT 2-6-2T 84013 just out of the paint shops at Crewe Works. JOHN GRIFFITHS

STANDARD 2MT 2-6-2T: ANOTHER IVATT UPGRADE

Also designed at Derby in 1953 was the Standard 2MT 2-6-2T, these were almost identical to HG Ivatt's LMS Class 2P 2MT 2-6-2Ts, which had appeared in 1946.

Modifications were made to the Ivatt design including a reduced cab to reduce the loading gauge and some standard fittings.

As most services that required 2MT 2-6-2Ts were already served by the 130 Ivatt engines, British Railways ordered only 30 engines, which eliminated ancient pre-Grouping steam locomotives as much as possible on local services. The first 20 were built at Crewe and the second batch of 10 at Darlington.

Also, Riddles favoured the use of steam push-pull sets rather than diesel multiple units, but was quite quickly overruled in this respect once BR's Modernisation Plan was published in 1955.

With DMUs seeing rapid and widespread introduction, no more of the Standard 2MT 2-6-2Ts were built. However, class members continued working push-pull trains right up to 1966.

moved to a similar position at Derby, succeeding H G Ivatt, but Harrison was not in favour of the disproportionate influence of LMS people on early BR locomotive policy. It was Harrison who was responsible for much of the design work on *Duke of Gloucester*, giving it Caprotti valve gear. Despite having a Britannia boiler and all the normal BR Standard features, No. 71000 clearly showed much Gresley LNER influence, being a three-cylinder Pacific.

It was the last new steam design for British Railways. Riddles' intention had been that it would be a big Britannia, with two cylinders, but this had proved impractical as the two cylinders would have had to be too big. The three-cylinder design was therefore forced on Riddles, who was reluctant to accept it in view of known problems with three-

cylinder Pacifics on the LNER. In the event it was the use of Caprotti valve gear that was the factor that allowed the project to go ahead.

Design of the draughting arrangements was subcontracted to Swindon, but despite advice to use a Kylchap exhaust system to deal with the sharp exhaust of Caprotti valve gear, Swindon fitted a standard double chimney, before Riddles could stop them, and it proved to be one of the design's Achilles heels.

Immediately after completion, it was displayed at a major exhibition of BR rolling stock at Willesden depot, organised for the International Railway Congress. The event was opened by the Duke of Gloucester, and so the unique 8P was named in his honour.

Never a popular engine, it nevertheless

came out of trials for thermal efficiency extremely well, but BR never honed it to perfection.

It was withdrawn in 1962 after only eight years, without having realised its true potential.

One of its outside cylinders was removed for display at the Science Museum, while the locomotive was sold as scrap to Woodham Brothers scrapyard at Barry in South Wales.

In 1974 a group of enthusiasts formed the Duke of Gloucester Steam Locomotive Trust, and spent 13 years restoring it to running order, at the Great Central Railway in Leicestershire. In preservation, some quite major design and construction faults were discovered and it is only in the heritage era that correction of these has allowed the engine to realise its full potential.

The completed *Duke of Gloucester* at Crewe Works in May 1954. BRITISH RAIL

BR Standard 9F No. 2-10-0 No. 92203, named *Black Prince* in preservation by owner the late David Shepherd, makes a flourishing departure from Kingsley & Froghall station on July 10, 2004, during a loan visit to the Churnet Valley Railway. It is now based permanently on the North Norfolk Railway. ROBIN JONES

STANDARD 9F 2-10-0: THE BEST OF THEM ALL?

The last in the series of BR Standard classes, the 9F was intended for use on fast, heavy long-distance freight workings.

Although the design was shared between Brighton and Doncaster in 1953, the 251 2-10-0s were built at Crewe and Swindon, and allocated to the ER, NER and LMR at first with the last batches going to the WR.

Externally similar to a Britannia Pacific, the actual design was very different, with few parts common to both classes; in fact the 9F has surprisingly little in common with any of the other Standard classes.

It was the ER's motive power officer, L P Parker, who made the case for a new design of powerful freight locomotive, able to shift heavy loads at fast speeds in round trips between distant destinations within the eight-hour shift of the footplate crew.

Riddles took up the challenge, initially designing a 2-8-2, but settled upon the 2-10-0 wheel arrangement for the increased traction and lower axle load that five-coupled axles can provide.

The centre driving wheels had no flanges, and those on the second and fourth coupled wheels were reduced in depth, to enable the locomotives to round curves more easily.

The 9F 2-10-0s were particularly successful, and indeed, many have said that they were the finest of all the Riddles' Standard designs. Although capable of the slow heavy freight haulage to be expected of Britain's most powerful steam engine, they were also capable of 90mph running.

Ten of the 9Fs built in 1955, Nos. 92020-92029, carried Franco-Crosti boilers. These incorporated a combustion gas feed water preheater that recuperated low-grade residual heat. In the 9F version, this took the form of a single cylindrical water drum running along the underside of the main boiler barrel. The standard chimney on top of the smokebox was only used during lighting up.

In normal working, the gases went through firetubes inside the preheater drum that led to a second smokebox situated beneath the boiler from which there was a second chimney on the right-hand side, just in front of the firebox. Although widely used in Italy, the system was not found to be particularly beneficial and did not justify the additional cost.

With a chimney right in front of the cab, footplate conditions were unpleasant and the second boilers and chimneys were quickly removed. The 10 locomotives remained very different in appearance to the rest of the class though, with no smoke deflectors and they lasted in service almost to the end of steam.

The last of the 999 BR Standards to be built was a 9F; No. 92220 was turned out from Swindon in May 1960, named *Evening Star* and painted in express lined green livery, something Riddles would have disapproved of.

Withdrawals started early as dieselisation took hold in many areas and there was little alternative use for the 9Fs. Nevertheless many lasted into 1968 and a few made it almost to the end of steam in August that year.

TRUE MASTERPIECE

Two of the new classes were purpose-built for the Western Region: the Class 4 4-6-0, was intended to do the same job as a Collett Manor, and the Standard 3 2-6-2T, superseding the likes of GWR prairies.

With his Standard 9F heavy freight 2-10-0s, Riddles produced a true masterpiece, even though the first did not appear until after he had left British Railways. Designed for hauling huge coal trains, these locomotives could be used in passenger service if required and were recorded as doing so at speeds of up to 90mph. They were markedly superior to the locomotives they replaced, and could pull far heavier trains than the 8F 2-8-0s.

A total of 251 were built, including the last locomotive of all constructed for British Railways. It may be deemed fitting that such an outstanding class should have the final word in British main line steam.

Robert Riddles retired in 1953 on the abolition of the Railway Executive, seven years before his last Standard was outshopped.

He became a director of Stothert & Pitt, cranemakers of Bath. He was replaced on the network by Roland Bond, who was appointed Chief

BELOW: An Up mineral at Barrow-on-Soar on May 17, 1962, is headed by BR 9F 2-10-0 No. 92134, which was built in June 1957, withdrawn in December 1966 and subsequently bought from preservation from Barry scrapyard. Allocated to Wellingborough, it worked heavy coal traffic on the Midland Main Line.
BEN BROOKSBANK*

Mechanical Engineer, BR Central Staff.

JF Harrison took over from Bond in 1958, but never had the opportunity to design new steam locomotives in this position and effectively took charge of the phasing out of BR steam. He retired on September 14, 1966.

Not long after Riddles' retirement, British Railways finally decided to proceed with the rapid conversion to diesel traction, as laid out in the Modernisation Plan of 1955. Many of the planned orders for BR Standard steam engines were cancelled.

Most were scrapped with years of useful life left in them.

SLOW TO IMPLEMENT MODERN TRACTION

Although the BR Standards were generally a success, there has been criticism of the policy pursued by Riddles. There were perfectly good engines still being produced by BR to Big Four designs and many of the Standard engines were not really necessary. BR

was also slow to implement modern traction, especially diesel multiple units, and to extend the LNER's main line electrification programme.

Riddles died on June on 1983. He would have witnessed the mess that the modernisation of British Railways had become, the terrific waste of resources by building steam locomotives and scrapping them with a few years, and the soaring losses made by the nationalised network that paved the way for the appointment of a business executive as British Railways chairman in 1961, in a desperate bid to make it profitable again.

The business executive's name: Dr Richard Beeching, a man synonymous with the vast pruning of loss-making rural branch lines and secondary routes, who oversaw the dying years of the steam era before it all came to an end on August 11, 1968. That was the date of the Liverpool to Carlisle and back 'Fifteen Guinea Special', the last steam train run on the main line by British Rail, finally closing the door on 166 years of history.

ABOVE: The last locomotive built in Britain for the main line was BR Standard 9F 2-10-0 No. 92220 *Evening Star,* which was ceremoniously unveiled at Swindon Works on March 18, 1960. Indeed, it was the only British main line steam locomotive earmarked for preservation from its date of construction. It was the 999th and last locomotive of the whole Riddles' Standard range. Furthermore, No. 92220 was the only 9F to be named, and liveried in lined passenger express BR Brunswick green as opposed to black. The name *Evening Star* was chosen following a competition run in 1959-60 by the Western Region Staff Magazine. There were three competition winners, driver T M Phillips (Aberystwyth), Boilermaker J S Sathi (Old Oak Common) and F L Pugh (Paddington), who had all suggested *Evening Star,* as a counterpoint to Isambard Kingdom Brunel's broad gauge *Morning Star.* No. 92220 was used over the Western Region and over the Somerset & Dorset Joint Railway line. Its main duties were as a heavy freight locomotive. However, No. 92220 was never just any locomotive, and its schedules were closely controlled to ensure that it returned home regularly for cleaning and maintenance in view of the special workings and exhibitions for which it was required to attend.It is seen on display outside the National Railway Museum in 2010. ROBIN JONES

CHAPTER 8

THE ENGLISH **E** ELECTRIC Co Ltd

THE 1948
EFFECT

BRITISH RAILWAYS

Nationalisation in 1948 may have saved Britain's railways from plunging into a downward spiral of unredeemable debt, but it was to prove uncharted territory in which a succession of costly errors of judgment were made.

A forerunner of the modern railway age: prototype Deltic DP1 outside Locomotion: The National Railway Museum at Shildon in October 2011. In 1954-55, a prototype locomotive incorporating two of the 18-cylinder Napier Deltic engines as used in Royal Navy minesweepers of the day was built at English Electric's Dick Kerr works in Preston. Owned by its builder, it was officially numbered DP1 (Diesel Prototype No. 1) and, finished in powder blue livery with cream stripes, carried the word Deltic in large capital letters on its sides. It distinctive front whiskers drew on the style of new American diesels, as English Electric was also thinking of the export market. A large continental-style lamp was fitted to the nose at either end. It underwent trials on the London Midland Region in October 1955, working between London and Liverpool, and also on the Settle and Carlisle line. Officials lost interest when it became clear that the West Coast Main Line was to be electrified, but the Eastern Region proved more welcoming, as nobody had, up to that stage, come up with a blueprint for a diesel that could better Gresley's Pacifics, especially the A4s. It ran successfully in trials on the Eastern Region, mainly between King's Cross and Doncaster, and British Railways was so impressed that it ordered 22 production versions. Sadly, DP1 suffered a serious powerplant failure in March 1961 and was taken out of service permanently, and preserved. ROBIN JONES

We have seen how state control of railways proved highly effective in both world wars, and indeed, by the start of the 1950s, British Railways was making a small working profit.

In 1954, Britain was one of only seven out of 17 major European countries whose railways were not 'in the red'.

However, the writing had long been on the wall, in the form of escalating completion from the more versatile and often cheaper motor transport. The following year, it recorded its first working loss.

As previously stated, the road haulage industry had bitterly opposed nationalisation by the Attlee government. Yet, under the Conservative government elected in 1951, road haulage was soon denationalised and deregulated. It could offer charges that greatly undercut those of rail, while the still-heavily regulated railways, which had to meet the extra burden of safety costs, remained under the control of the British Transport Commission.

Britain, the originator of the self-propelled railway locomotive, was entrenched in years of postwar austerity, and by then was lagging behind North America and several European countries in moving from steam to diesel and electric traction. The shortage of public resources was, as stated before, the primary factor, but in addition, Clement Attlee did not want to reduce the demand for British coal and cause unemployment in the newly nationalised pits, while Robert Riddles added that home-produced coal was far cheaper than imported diesel fuel. Only the Southern Region, by virtue of its suburban lines in London, operated a large number of trains not hauled by steam.

Measures were taken to enhance the performance of prewar locomotives working in postwar conditions: for example, the Western Region equipped all the King 4-6-0s and many Castle 4-6-0s with double chimneys to improve their steaming; many of Bulleid's streamlined Pacifics were rebuilt without their distinctive air-smooth casings and all of the Gresley Pacifics had been fitted with Kylchap blastpipes and double chimneys, a move especially effective with the A3s. Despite the excellence of many of Riddles' Standard designs, history records that they were just a stop gap, with their days numbered as the UK economy began to recover and was able to afford modernisation.

In 1954, the Leeds/Bradford area of the West Riding of Yorkshire was chosen by British Railways as a pilot area in which to test the first of its diesel multiple units, a descendant of the GWR diesel railcars, and previous LMS experimental vehicles. Also, in June that year, the electrified Woodhead route between Manchester and Sheffield, a project first proposed by the LNER, was completed, with the electric services inaugurated that September.

By the mid-Fifties, British Railways was losing out to the road and air haulage business, and a review was ordered.

Western Region diesel hydraulic Class 52 D1062 *Western Courier* on display on the turntable at Minehead on the West Somerset Railway on June 12, 2009. An impressive machine, certainly, but because no other British Railways' region went for diesel hydraulics, their operations were restricted outside former GWR territory as there were few facilities for servicing and footplate crews were unfamiliar with them. ROBIN JONES

A Derby lightweight diesel multiple unit at Keswick on June 25, 1957. The introduction of DMUs proved successful in many areas, and were welcomed by many passengers, but they could not prevent the closure of many rural lines, including that of Keswick. COLOUR-RAIL

THE MODERNISATION PLAN

On December 1, 1954, British Railways unveiled its blueprint for the future, in a report entitled Modernisation and Re-Equipment of the British Railways. In it, British Railways set out its strategy to compete against road transport, by increasing speed, reliability, safety and line capacity, while making services more attractive to both passengers and freight operators.

The most marked feature of the plan was the aim to completely eradicate steam locomotives and replace them with diesel and electric alternatives. It also proposed the electrification of principal main lines, including the East Coast Main Line to Leeds and possibly York, the Great Northern suburban system; Euston to Birmingham/Manchester/ Liverpool; Chelmsford to Clacton/Ipswich/Felixstowe; the Liverpool Street north-east suburban

system; Fenchurch Street to Tilbury and Shoeburyness; and the Glasgow north suburban network.

The report also proposed a new fleet of passenger and freight rolling stock, the creation of large goods marshalling yards with automated shunting to streamline freight handling, mass resignalling and track renewal, and the closure of more unprofitable lines and duplicated routes. The report proposed to spend £1240 million over 15 years to achieve these goals.

In 1956, a government White Paper confidently stated that modernisation would help eliminate BR's financial deficit by 1962.

At the time, British Railways was still building large numbers of steam locomotives, and rushed into assorting a wide selection of diesels, which outside manufacturers were only too happy to supply. This first-generation modern

traction met with varying degrees of success; however, some of the diesel classes would end up being withdrawn even before the last steam locomotives disappeared from the main line. It all looked good on paper, but the reality proved very different.

The regions were, by and large, still being run by Big Four management, and had a certain amount of autonomy. This factor was apparent in the Western Region's choice of diesels.

Just as the GWR had gone it alone with Isambard Kingdom Brunel's 7ft 0¼in broad gauge when everywhere outside its area had adopted George Stephenson's 4ft 8½in standard gauge, so its successor the Western Region chose diesel-hydraulic locomotives as opposed to the diesel-electric types favoured elsewhere. Yes, some of these, like the Class 52 Westerns and Class 42 Warships, turned in very impressive performances, while others, for example, the North British Locomotive Company's Type 2 Bo-Bos often failed to impress meaning this class had become extinct by 1971. For the sake of standardisation, just as the last broad gauge lines had been converted in 1892, so British Railways decided to phase diesel-hydraulics out from the Sixties onwards in pursuit of standardisation, but not before colossal amounts of taxpayers' money had been wasted. The last Westerns ran in British Rail ownership in 1977.

THE PLAN FALLS SHORT

The haphazard stab at modernisation that marked the twilight years of steam did not, as everyone was promised, improve matters. The Modernisation Plan sought to upgrade the existing railway network, but did not take into account rapidly shifting demand from its customers.

Steam locomotives were replaced on a like-for-like basis by diesels, at a time when customers for mixed-goods trains

PROGRESS   Every week British Railways Modernisation Plan goes further ahead

A British Railways' poster extolling the virtues of the Modernisation Plan.

One of the least-successful of the diesels ordered under the Modernisation Plan were the Class 8 Metropolitan Vickers Co-Bos. Twenty were ordered and built between 1958-59, but their Crossley engines gave problems and the last was withdrawn as early as 1969. One of them, D5705, survived by being used for a test train and then as a heating unit, and is now preserved. ROBIN JONES

Last summer of the Midland & Great Northern: Midland 3F 0-6-0 No. 44231 passes the signal bracket as it crosses the River Great Ouse at South Lynn with the 8am Chesterfield to Yarmouth Beach train on August 30, 1958. The section between Kelling Heath near Holt and Sheringham was reopened as the North Norfolk Railway. The section from Sheringham to Cromer remained open as part of the national network. HUGH BALLANTYNE

on branch lines were switching to roads, and branch lines were themselves closing.

The nationalised network's annual working deficit in 1956 was £16.5 million: by 1962 it had reached more than £100 million. Overall, the promised return on investment failed to materialise.

The failure of the Modernisation Plan led to a distrust of British Railways' financial planning abilities by the Treasury, which was to haunt the nationalised railway for the rest of its existence. The plan had promised that in return of expenditure of more than £1240 million, traffic levels would increase, and the network would be back in profit by 1962. However, the opposite happened. Losses rose to £68 million in 1960 to £87 million in 1961, £104 million in 1962, and the British Transport Commission could no longer

pay the interest on its loans. By 1961 losses were running at £300,000 a day.

The very modest programme of early Nationalisation closures continued in 1949 with passenger services withdrawn between Liverpool Lime Street to Alexandra Dock, Stratford-upon-Avon to Broom, and Fenchurch Street to Stratford (Bow Junction).

In 1950, a total of 150 route miles was closed, rising to 275 in 1951 and 300 in 1952. The figure dipped again to 275 miles in 1953, and a total of 500 miles was closed between 1954-57. A further 150 miles were lost in 1958.

The biggest shock came in 1959, with the closure of a complete system in the form of the Midland & Great Northern Joint Railway lines apart from a few piecemeal sections such as Cromer to Melton Constable and North Walsham to Mundesley, on February 28.

For many railwaymen, the loss of

such a large slice on the network showed that the writing was on the wall.

The loss of most of the Midland & Great Northern's 186 route miles brought the total length lost to the network in 1959 to 350. Another 175 miles followed in 1960, 150 in 1961 and a whopping 780 in 1962. In fairness, some of the lines closed during the 1950s removed obvious route duplication, but others reflected the public's changing choice of transport at a time when increasingly there was more money around.

Since Nationalisation in 1948, railway staff numbers had fallen 26% from 648,000 to 474,000, the number of railway wagons had fallen 29% from 1,200,000 to 848,000, and around 3000 miles had been lost. If the unions in the late Forties had seen that coming, would they have supported state ownership? But had the Big Four remained in place, would it have been even worse?

New generation: Class 31 Brush Type 2 A1A-A1A diesel D5504 at Beccles on July 19, 1958. COLOUR RAIL

THE 1955 RAIL STRIKE

The shift from steam to diesel and electric traction was a worldwide phenomenon, as was the closure of unprofitable and lesser-used cross-country routes and branch lines in the face of cheaper road transport. However, there were also local factors that exacerbated the decline of railway network in the Fifties.

Historians have often pointed to the national rail strike of 1955 as a watershed moment for British Railways.

During the 1950s, as the austerity years faded and the British economy boomed, trade unions became stronger. Backed by the threat of strike action, unions found themselves able to demand better wages and working conditions for their members.

Days after Anthony Eden's Conservative government won a general election victory, train drivers' union ASLEF, the Associated Society of Locomotive Engineers and Firemen, called a strike over a pay claim, demanding a rise that amounted to the price of an extra packet of cigarettes a week.

The May 28-June 14 strike brought British industry to a standstill, although locomen who belonged to the National Union of Railwaymen continued to work. British Railways still managed to convey a quarter of its normal passenger traffic and a third of its freight, but as far as the public was concerned, there was no going back.

The strike necessitated a mass switch by both passengers and freight customers from rail to road. By then, road transport was now far more commonplace than ever before, and many customers did not return to the railways after the strike ended. Pick-up goods services were hit hard in the aftermath of the strike.

Few had predicted the severity of the outcome, and the dispute cost around £12 million in lost revenue. You cannot blame unions for fighting on behalf of their members, but by the Fifties there was widening condemnation that their leaders were failing to exercise their power responsibly and judiciously.

The inability of the Modernisation Plan to claw back the promised £85 million a year, coupled with a desire to prevent the country ever being held to ransom again, saw government transport policy finally shift from rail to road.

MR MOTORWAY JOINS THE FRAY

The Conservative party was returned to power in the October 1959 general election, and former Postmaster General Ernest Marples, the man who had introduced postcodes to Britain, was appointed minister of transport, a post he held until October 16, 1964.

Qualified accountant Marples founded Marples-Ridgway, a construction firm that built many roads, soon demonstrated his preference for spending public money on motorways rather than investing in railways.

In 1959, he approved the first inter-city British motorway, the M1. Britain's first section of motorway, the eight-mile Preston bypass, the first part of the M6 to be completed, was opened on December 5, 1958. He also introduced parking meters, yellow lines and seat belts.

Marples opened the first section of the M1, between Junction 5 (Watford) and Junction 18 (Crick/Rugby) on November 2, 1959.

To avoid a conflict of interest, he undertook to sell his controlling shareholder interest in his road construction company as soon as he became transport minister, although there was a purchaser's requirement that he buy back the shares after he ceased to hold office, at the original price, should the purchaser so require. It was later revealed that he had sold his shares to his wife.

So here we had the man who held the future of the national rail network in his hands very closely connected with a major financial interest in road building.

As transport minister, his first move was to impose tighter control over the British Transport Commission and call a halt to the excesses of the Modernisation Plan.

In early 1960, the British Transport Commission was told that any

Minister of Transport Ernest Marples, who had huge private interests in building motorways and trust roads.

investment project that involved spending more than $250,000 would have to be cleared with the Ministry, the ultimate decision resting with Marples.

By then, the winds had changed in Whitehall. Far from the optimism for the rail network of January 1, 1948, in government circles there was a growing belief that railways were an expensive and increasingly outmoded legacy from Victorian times. What was the purpose in propping up lossmaking lines with public money when new roads were being built to do the same job but more efficiently?

On March 10, 1960, at the start of the parliamentary debate on the Guillebaud Report into public-sector spending, Prime Minister Harold Macmillan said: "The carriage of minerals, including coal, an important traffic for the railways, has gone down. At the same time, there has been an increasing use of road transport in all its forms.

"The industry must be of a size and pattern suited to modern conditions and prospects. In particular, the railway system must be remodelled to meet current needs, and the modernisation plan must be adapted to this new shape.

"Secondly, the public must accept the need for changes in the size and pattern of the industry. This will involve certain sacrifices of convenience, for example, in the reduction of uneconomic services."

RAILWAYMAN OR SURGEON?

On March 10, 1961, Marples told the House of Commons that one Dr Richard Beeching, technical director of ICI, and a name not yet known to the public, would become the first chairman of the new British Railways Board from June 1 that year. Beeching would receive the same yearly salary that he was earning at ICI, the controversial sum of $24,000 (more than $490,000 by the 2016 equivalent), which was $14,000 more than that of Prime Minister Harold Macmillan.

Under the Transport Act of 1962, Harold Macmillan's Conservative government dissolved the British Transport Commission, having created the board to take over its railway duties from January 1, 1963.

The new board was directed under Section 22 of the Act to run the railways so that its operating profits were "not less than sufficient" for meeting the running costs.

This clause marked a major first for British railway legislation and was a turning point for the system. From then onwards, each railway service should pay for itself or at least show that it had the possibility of doing so. The days of mass subsidy, with profitable services supporting the unprofitable ones, and the taxpayer footing the bill if the overall figures did not tally would soon

cause him to be regarded in circles as a surgeon rather than a railwayman."

SHARPENING AN AXE

The 1962 Act also introduced new legislation for the closure of railway lines. Section 56(7) ruled that British Railways should give at least six weeks' notice of its intention to close a line and to publish the proposal in two local newspapers in the area affected for two successive weeks.

Each notice would have to provide the proposed closure dates, details of alternative public transport, including services that British Railways was to lay on as a result of closure, and inviting objections within the six-week period to a specified address.

A copy of the notice was also to be sent to the relevant Area Transport Users Consultative Committee, which would receive objections from affected rail users, and submit a report to the minister of transport.

The Central Transport Consultative Committee was a new body that replaced a similar one established under the Transport Act 1947, which had nationalised the railways, and was intended to represent railway consumers. The Area Transport Users Consultative Committees were additional bodies set up to cover local areas.

It would be the job of the Area Committees to look at the hardship, which it considered would be caused as a result of the closure, and recommend measures to ease that hardship.

A line closure would not go ahead until the Area Committee had reported to the transport minister and he had given his consent to it. Based on the Area Committee's report, the minister could subject his consent to closure to certain conditions, such as the provision of alternative transport services.

Dr Richard Beeching holds up a copy of his 1963 report, The Reshaping of British Railways, which spelled the death knell for thousands of miles of loss-making lines and provoked a wave of public anger and protests. NRM

However, the minister was not legally obliged to adhere to any of the Area Committee's recommendations, and therefore there was no safeguard by which public feeling could take priority over policy.

Among the first lines endorsed by Beeching for full closure was the Helston branch, where, ironically, the Great Western Railway had pioneered the use of buses.

Local people had seen closures elsewhere in the late Fifties and for years had believed that the writing was on the wall for the line.

When the end for passenger services came on November 3, 1962, it was one of the first acts carried out under the auspices of new British Railways chairman. Even dieselisation could not save it from becoming the first of the Cornish branch lines to close.

DAY OF RECKONING

As we have seen, rail closures had been enacted since the 1930s, as motor transport gained more ground. The steadily rolling snowball had gathered momentum since Nationalisation, years before Beeching was appointed.

The seminal moment came on March 27, 1963, when Beeching's report, The Reshaping of British Railways, was published.

Long before then, seasoned railwaymen had seen traffic dwindle to a trickle or nothing on many lines and knew that closures were inevitable.

Yet the publication of a report detailing wholesale slaughter of much of the network was still met with absolute horror.

To the public, who had no grasp of railway finances, and had always

accepted that the railways 'would always be there', the following day's headlines enshrined Beeching as the man who took 'their' line away. Indeed, Beeching has often been referred to as the most hated civil servant of all time.

His 148-page report called for a third of the rail network to be closed and ripped up, and was immediately dubbed the 'Beeching Axe' by the press.

The title stuck.

Out of around 18,000 route miles, 5000 of them, mainly cross-country routes and rural branches, should close completely, it recommended.

In the past, it was predominantly rural branches serving areas of low population that were closed. This time round, trunk routes were listed; the Somerset & Dorset Joint Railway

system, the Waverley Route from Carlisle to Edinburgh, the Great Central Railway from Nottingham to Marylebone, as well as passenger services on the Settle and Carlisle route.

Over and above all this, many other lines were to lose their passenger services and remain open for freight only, while intermediate stations serving small communities on main lines should close, in order to speed up inter-city trains.

In all, a total of 2363 stations and halts were to be axed, including 435 under consideration before Beeching's report appeared, of which 235 had already been closed.

The sweeping changes to the network should be implemented in a seven-year programme, the report recommended.

BEECHING'S FORMULA

The core basis of the report was the premise that said railways should be used to meet that part of the national transport requirement for which they offered the best available means, and stop trying to compete in areas where they were now ill-suited, when faced with competition from cars, buses and lorries.

A key study into traffic flows on all UK rail routes had been carried out during the week ending April 23, 1962, two weeks after Easter, and found that 30% of route miles carried only 1% one of passengers and freight, and half of all stations contributed only 2% of revenue.

Furthermore, half the total route mileage carried only 4% of the total passenger miles, and 5% of the freight ton miles, revenue from them amounting to £20 million with the costs doubling that figure. Such figures did not stack up, nor, it seemed, were ever likely to again.

From the least-used half of the stations the gross revenue from all traffic did not even cover the cost of the stations themselves, and made no contribution to route costs, movement or terminal costs.

The statistics showed that it was doubtful if the income from up to 6000 passengers a week on branch lines covered movement costs alone, and clearly money would be saved by withdrawing services over them.

The report stated that overall, passenger traffic on a single-track branch line added around £1750 a mile to the cost of route maintenance, signalling and the staffing of stations.

Therefore, a passenger density below 10,000 could not be considered as economic, even where freight traffic absorbed a proportion of the route cost.

Where there was no other traffic, 17,000 passengers per week might make a branch line pay its way.

Even the provision of diesel railbuses – a cost-cutting measure introduced on many branches in the late Fifties as a key element of a drive to prune staffing levels and increase efficiency – demanded a passenger density of 14,000 a week, as against 17,000 a week with full-blown diesel multiple units.

At the start of his report, Beeching said that, "there had never before been any systematic assembly of a basis of information upon which planning could be founded, and without which the proper role of the railways in the transport system as a whole could not be determined."

Indeed, closures had previously been undertaken in individual regions, without reference to their impact on the national system. Furthermore, several of the routes listed in the report had already been proposed for closure by their regions, and Beeching merely confirmed those decisions.

In a scene typical of 'last day' trains on branch lines closed by Beeching, BR Standard 2MT 2-6-2T No. 84015 waits to leave on September 25, 1965. Coal traffic lasted until July 30 the following year. HUGH BALLANTYNE

Beeching may be seen as having merely streamlined the decision-making processes that had gone before, with a universal set of criteria. He did not implement any closures himself – the final decision was made in Whitehall. Ernest Marples employed him and instructed him, and Beeching was "only obeying orders".

The report claimed that its suggested measures should eradicate the network's deficit by 1970 – another promise of a golden age to come, just as in the Modernisation Plan eight years before.

Needless to say, the many communities set to become disenfranchised by the rail network as a result of the closures were immediately outraged. Not every family had, by 1963, the luxury of owning a car, and hardships would inevitably result in the cause of balancing the British Railways' books.

The report stated: "Immediately prior to the war, in 1938, the number of private cars registered was 1,944,000. In 1954 there were 3,100,000, and in 1961 there were 6,000,000. By 1970 it is expected that there will be a total of 13,000,000 cars registered, equivalent to 24.3 per 100 of the population or 76 per 100 families."

However, the sheer scale of the Beeching cuts, coming on top of 780 miles closed in 1962 and another 324 in 1964, led to nationwide anger, from rail users, local residents, civic representatives and the unions.

Protest marches were held, councils voted against closure, MPs were lobbied, accounts were disseminated to provide fresh arguments that certain lines could be made viable, but in most cases to no

avail. Regardless of widening public disdain, the Conservative government accepted Beeching's report after it was debated in the House of Commons in April 1963. It promised that axed rail services would be replaced by cheaper and more flexible bus services.

In 1958, the boundaries of the regions had been redrawn to make them geographical rather than based on Big Four ownership.

So, we saw former LMS lines in Yorkshire transferred from the London Midland to the Eastern and North Eastern regions: the London Midland Region gained the former Great Central Railway lines outside Yorkshire and Lincolnshire from the Eastern Region in return.

Former LMS lines in the south-west of the country, including the northern section of the Somerset & Dorset Joint Railway, were transferred to the Western Region.

The process continued thereafter, in 1963, the Southern Region's 'Withered Arm' network in Devon and Cornwall was transferred to the Western Region. Not only was any last remaining vestige of competition eradicated, but it made it easier for routes deemed to 'double up' to be weeded out. The Western Region main line to Penzance served large centres of population such as Exeter, Plymouth and Truro, while the 'Withered Arm' and its myriad offshoots ran through large tracts of sparsely populated countryside and served small towns or seaside resorts. If one had to go, it may have seemed a clear choice, but it was often said that the Western men settled old scores in closing Southern lines.

NEW MEN FOR A NEW AGE

It was not only Britain's railways that were faced with a period of radical change. The old order of politics and government was about to undergo a seismic upheaval.

Prime Minister Harold Macmillan, who to many represented the 'old establishment', resigned on the grounds of ill health – since held to have been a misdiagnosis of prostate cancer – on October 18, 1963, during the Conservative party conference.

In its final year, the credibility of his government had been damaged by two scandals. Firstly, there was the Vassall spy affair.

British civil servant William Vassall had, because of his homosexuality, been blackmailed by the USSR into spying, and had been sentenced to 18 years in jail once discovered. That scandal was later eclipsed by the Profumo affair. Secretary of State for War John Profumo had lied to the House of Commons about his affair with Christine Keeler, said to have been the mistress of an alleged Russian spy.

Foreign Secretary Alec Douglas-Home took over as prime minister, but the Profumo affair had so badly damaged the Conservative government that it was incapable of being saved by a 60-year-old aristocrat who had been titled Lord Home until renouncing his title under the 1963 Peerages Act.

By contrast, the Labour party was newly led in 1963 by Harold Wilson, a comparative youngster at 46, who promised a new age of achievement and prosperity. His party boldly promised to reverse all of Beeching's cuts if it gained

A luxury Midland Pullman set heads north out of St Pancras. Using two new Blue Pullman six-car diesel-electric units, it was launched in July 1960 in a bid to make rail travel fashionable again, an all-first-class service aimed at covering the high end of the Manchester-London business market. SHIPLEY43*

power, and sack him into the bargain. Thirteen years of Conservative rule ended when Labour won the 1964 general election with a four-seat majority, and seeking a bigger majority after 18 months, a second election in March 1966 returned Labour 96 seats clear of its rivals.

History records that the new Labour government did not sack the British Railways' chairman or reverse his cuts. On the contrary, it kept him in place and not only implemented his recommended cuts but went on to make more of its own.

In 1964, the first year that many of the Beeching report's recommendations were implemented, 1058 miles were closed, followed by 600 in 1965, in the first year of the Wilson administration.

In December 1965, *The Railway Magazine*'s correspondent Onlooker, pleading for a square deal for the railways after what he called a "year of frustration", commented: "The Reshaping report listed 267 passenger services to be withdrawn and 2363 stations and halts to be closed. Over 300 parliamentary constituencies were affected, yet not a single Tory MP voted against its approval.

"Also, since changing sides in the House, not a single Labour MP has had the courage to remind the Party's leaders about this unredeemed pledge."

In 1966, another 750 miles were closed, followed by 300 miles in 1967, 400 in 1968, 250 in 1969 and 275 in 1970. Only then did the rate of closures rapidly f all off.

So, while Ernest Marples, the road-building minister who appointed Beeching and rubber stamped many, though not all, of his recommended closures, it was Labour – the party that had nationalised the railways – that adhered the same policy once elected, when it found that it too had to make unpopular decisions in the face of the soaring British Railways' deficit and growth in car ownership.

Labour Prime Minister Harold Wilson. Before his 1964 election victory, his party pledged to sack Beeching and reverse his cuts.

Harold Macmillan, who quit in 1963 following two scandals, came to be seen as representative of the old order from which the public would demand change.

BLUE IS THE COLOUR

While the Big Four companies had their own distinctive corporate liveries for locomotives and rolling stock, British Railways stumbled somewhat on early attempts at a uniform livery. The different regions, inheritors of Big Four traditions that died hard, often disagreed.

The standard livery for most British Railways' steam locomotives was black, while express passenger locomotives were painted in the Great Western colours of Brunswick green, with orange and black lining. In earlier years, British Railways painted its express passenger locomotives in blue livery, but it failed as it highlighted dirt and grime at every available opportunity.

First-generation diesel locomotives and multiple units mostly appeared in green livery too. As part of a plan to find a suitable corporate livery for the new

FREIGHT: A SUCCESS STORY

Many people think of Beeching as the man who got rid of the nation's beloved steam trains and wanted to close as much of the system as he could. However, one of his big success stories is so often overlooked, freight.

His strategy was to lead road transport do what they did best, and the same with railways.

The introduction of cost-effective 'Merry-Go-Round' coal trains and Freightliner container services allowed

rail to once again offer serious competition to road haulage when it came to bulk loads. A train of MGR wagons is able to load and unload its cargo while still moving – thereby maximising efficiency of the wagon fleet.

When 'Merry-Go-Round' services were first introduced, British Rail designed an all-new wagon with air brakes and the capacity to carry 33 tons of pulverised coal.

With investment from the Central

Electricity Generating Board and the National Coal Board, new power stations were built at Aberthaw, Drax, Didcot, Eggborough, Fiddlers Ferry and Ratcliffe to handle MGR traffic, while several existing power stations were converted to MGR operation.

The Freightliner concept, borrowed by Beeching from an American model, involves the use of reusable intermodal or shipping containers (commonly known as ISO containers) for moving products and raw materials between locations or countries.

As part of Beeching's rationalisation drive, British Railways introduced a system whereby ISO containers were carried on flat wagons between a series of dedicated inland terminals, using gantry cranes for transhipment between road and rail.

Beeching originally intended Freightliner to handle domestic goods traffic, but this volume was soon surpassed by freight between deep-sea ports, such as Southampton Maritime and inland distribution terminals like Dudley, opened on the site of the town's closed station in 1967, becoming one of the most profitable in the country.

In 1995, Freightliner was privatised as a stand-alone company when its own management bought it out.

One of the original Freightliner containers preserved at the National Railway Museum. Freightliner was one of Beeching's big success stories. ROBIN JONES

In a scene typical of anywhere on the 'all blue and white' national network of the late Sixties and Seventies, Class 37 No. 37043 departs from Liverpool Street on May 3, 1976. BARRY LEWIS*

Oswestry was once a hub of several lines, but lost all its passenger services under the Beeching Axe. The Cambrian Railways main line to Welshpool was closed on January 18, 1965, and passenger services to Gobowen ended on November 7, 1966. GWR 4-6-0 No. 7815 *Fritwell Manor* heads a Down stopping train at Oswestry. The locomotive was withdrawn on October 31, 1964. WAGON 16*

diesel and electric fleet and coaching stock, several experimental colours were tried.

Shortly after Nationalisation it was decided that all coaches should be painted in a two-tone livery of carmine and cream for corridor coaches, with all-over crimson, very much as successor to the LMS livery, being used for local, non-corridor stock, to give a traditional 'feel' while differing from any of the Big Four company liveries. In the Fifties, the regions were allowed to revert to liveries of their choice, with the most independent of them, the Western Region, readopting GWR chocolate and cream, while the Southern Region reverted to malachite green.

Beeching decided that British Railways needed a major rebranding, from the locomotives and stock down to staff uniforms, station signs and even tableware, seat rest covers and official letterheads.

An exhibition, 'The New Face of British Railways', was staged at the Design Centre in London from January 4-23, 1965, with the aim of launching British Railways' corporate identity.

Everything was to be painted in monastral blue and pearl grey, set off by flame red.

From the outset, locomotives kept the small yellow front warning panels from the green livery era, until the British Railways Board's accident prevention service ordered that the yellow was to cover the entire front of the cabs in order to make locomotives more visible to trackside staff for safety reasons.

From that year, British Railways traded as British Rail; the name change being another aspect of its corporate identity makeover.

IT COULD HAVE BEEN WORSE

In February 1965, British Railways published a second Beeching report, titled The Development of the Major Railway Trunk Routes.

Nicknamed "Beeching II", the report picked out routes that would justify large-scale investment to handle projected increases in both passenger and freight traffic over the next two decades. At first reading, the new report appeared highly positive, with major investment in a series of identified key routes. However, many critics immediately saw this as 'spin', masking the fact that the routes not chosen for upgrading would inevitably end up being closed.

Beeching denied that more drastic closures were top of his new agenda in the closing paragraphs of the conclusion to the new report.

He was then asked by the government to undertake a new job, carrying out a study to integrate Britain's entire transport system, echoing the aims of the Attlee regime when it nationalised all of Britain's transport in 1948.

He had said he was willing to carry out the task but could devote no more than six months to it, as he intended to return to ICI as agreed. However, Beeching and the government could not agree terms despite much discussion, and the new job offer was withdrawn.

So, a year before his five-year leave of absence from ICI was due to expire, he left British Railways on May 31, 1965. It has never satisfactorily resolved as to whether he left of his own accord or was sacked.

In a statement to the House of Commons, Transport Minister Tom Fraser said: "Since it is Dr Beeching's desire to return to ICI by the middle of next year, I have come to the conclusion that it would not be practicable for him to carry out the sort of study the government wants, in the way in which we think it should be done, during the time which he could devote to it."

However, Frank Cousins, the Labour minister of technology, told the Commons in November 1965 that Beeching had been sacked by Fraser.

Beeching was replaced as British Railways' chairman by Stanley Raymond, later Sir Stanley Raymond, who had joined the Western Region as divisional manager in 1962 and impressed by cutting losses. He also backed away from many of the recommendations made in the 1965 report.

It had become increasingly apparent that not only had the rail closures not produced anything like the promised savings or ended the British Railways' deficit but were unlikely ever to do so.

Steam locomotives withdrawn en masse ended up at scrapyards around the country, where they were often cut up within days. The most famous of them all was the Woodham Brothers yard at Barry in South Wales (pictured in July 1968), where owner Dai Woodham made the decision to concentrate on the more profitable scrapping of wagons and save the engines for a rainy day. As a result, 213 of them survived long enough to be bought for railway preservation purposes. HUGH LLEWELYN*

Landmark moment: on August 11, 1968, *Oliver Cromwell* passes Ais Gill with 1T57, the fabled 'Fifteen Guinea Special' enthusiasts' charter, which had ended British Railways' main line steam haulage. ALAN BROWN

THE SOCIAL FACTOR

Barbara Castle was appointed as transport minister on December 23, 1965, and oversaw the closure of around 2050 miles of railway lines both under the Beeching plan along with routes that he had not suggested, such as Buxton to Matlock, and so her appointment was hardly a reversal of policy.

Under her 1968 Transport Act, she importantly introduced a new social factor into legislation regarding such closures, and a further 3500 miles were given the possibility of a reprieve.

Section 39 of the 1968 Act introduced the first government subsidies for such lines. Grants could be paid where three conditions were met.

Firstly, the line had to be unremunerative. Secondly, it was desirable for social or economic reasons for the passenger services to continue, and thirdly, it was financially unreasonable to expect British Rail to provide those services without a grant.

Mrs Castle saved several individual routes including branch lines; York to Harrogate, Manchester to Buxton, Oxenholme to Windermere, Exeter to Exmouth and in Cornwall, the Looe branch and the St Ives line.

She wrote off more than a billion pounds of British Rail's debt, and introduced the means whereby which both national and regional government would be able to subsidise lossmaking parts of the network that nonetheless provided wider social and economic benefits.

The 1968 Act saved several branch lines from closure, but some, like the Waverley Route and the Barnstaple-Ilfracombe line still did not quality under criteria and were axed. Furthermore, the Varsity Line that linked the university cities of Oxford and Cambridge saw services withdrawn from the Oxford-Bletchley section and the Bedford-Cambridge section at the end of 1967, even though the line had not been listed for closure in Beeching's 1963 report.

Ironically, by the time the 1968 Act had been passed, many lines and services that would have qualified for subsidies had already been closed, making it a case of too little too late.

Mrs Castle's approach to subsiding railways has continued to this day.

A delegation of Waverley Route protestors in London in December 1968, with a young David Steel MP, the future Liberal Democrat leader in the centre. However, people power was not enough to persuade the government to change its mind, and the 98-mile Carlisle to Edinburgh trunk route saw its last trains on January 5 the following year. After decades of clamouring by local people to reopen it, the northern section between Edinburgh to Tweedbank was rebuilt as the Borders Railway and reopened on September 6, 2015, with an official opening by Queen Elizabeth II three days later.

Transport Minister Barbara Castle introduced key legislation that allowed loss-making lines to receive a subsidy provided they could be shown to be of social importance, but nonetheless closed routes over and above those Beeching had recommended. PASSENGER TRANSPORT EXECUTIVE GROUP.

Class 125 InterCity sector-liveried High Speed Train at Eaton Crossing, a foot crossing on the East Coast Main Line to the south of Retford. The InterCity 125 was one of the greatest success stories of motive power under Nationalisation, and indeed in the history of Britain's railways. Class 125 High Speed Trains were introduced in 1976 and most of them are still in front-line revenue-earning service. PHIL SANGWELL*

THE SEVENTIES AND BEYOND

By the early Seventies, the map of the British Rail network looked very much as it does today. One shock closure on January 5, 1970 was that of the 1500V DC electrified Woodhead Route between Sheffield and Manchester. The electrification had been completed in 1955 when the upgraded line was opened amid a blaze of publicity.

Its closure, for which Beeching was not responsible, came after it was decided that the alternative Hope Valley line through Edale would be stay open instead, for social and network reasons, and would accommodate all Manchester-Sheffield passenger traffic.

One of the last Beeching closures to be implemented was the GWR branch from Maiden Newton on the main line to Weymouth to Bridport, in May 1975.

In the north of England, the Haltwhistle-Alston branch in the Pennines had survived Beeching's closure recommendation because of the lack of an all-weather road as an alternative, but the last train ran on May 1, 1976. By then the network had shrunk to 12,000 miles of track and 2000 stations, around the same size it is now.

On July 6, 1985, the line from Eridge to Tunbridge Wells was closed, in accordance with a Beeching recommendation.

In 1983 Sir David Serpell, a civil servant who had worked with Beeching, compiled what became known as the Serpell Report, which called for more drastic rail closures. The report was met with fierce resistance from many quarters, and it was quickly abandoned by Margaret Thatcher's Conservative government.

While passenger levels decreased steadily from the late Fifties to the late Seventies, there was an upsurge with the introduction of the high-speed Intercity 125 trains in the late 1970s and early 1980s.

British Railways had first used the term Inter-City in 1950 as the name of a train running between Paddington and Wolverhampton Low Level.

In 1966, British Rail made Inter-City in 1966 a brand name for all of its long-haul express passenger services.

The Eighties saw severe cuts in government funding and above-inflation increases in fares, but services became more cost-effective.

In 1986 the British Railways Board divided its operations into a number of sectors (sectorisation). The sector responsible for long-distance express trains assumed the brand name InterCity, which afterwards became profitable. Indeed, InterCity became one of Britain's top 150 companies operating city centre to city centre travel across the nation.

Electrification, a cornerstone of the Modernisation Plan, finally made its mark in the Eighties.

The Thatcher government, which had been widely considered to be anti-rail, authorised the electrification of the East Coast Main Line including the line from Doncaster to Leeds from 1985, with the work completed in 1991.

Network SouthEast undertook numerous electrification projects, including the Midland Main Line to Bedford and the Southern 750 V

DC system reached Hastings and Weymouth. Electrification in East Anglia included the line from London Liverpool Street to Norwich and also to King's Lynn.

The Chiltern Main Line was extensively modernised to open up an additional link between Marylebone and rebuilt Birmingham Snow Hill, and its services were successfully launched in 1987.

And what of Ernest Marples, the man behind the Beeching cuts?

He retired from the House of Commons at the February 1974 general election. Three months later, his public service was rewarded when he was made a life peer as Baron Marples of Wallasey.

In early 1975, before the end of the tax year, Marples fled without warning by night ferry to the tax haven of Monaco, with his belongings packed into tea chests, after fighting off a reassessment of his financial assets.

It was said that he had formulated a plot to remove £2-million from Britain through his Liechtenstein company. He claimed he had been asked to pay unpaid tax dating back three decades.

After he had gone, discarded clothes and possessions were found scattered on the floors of his Belgravia home.

The Government froze Marples' remaining assets in Britain for the next 10 years, but most of his fortune had by then been squirreled away to Monaco and Lichtenstein.

He never returned to Britain, and spent the rest of his life in his French chateau at Fleurie, where he owned a vineyard, dying on July 6, 1978.

CHAPTER 9

THE FIRST
PRIVATISATIONS

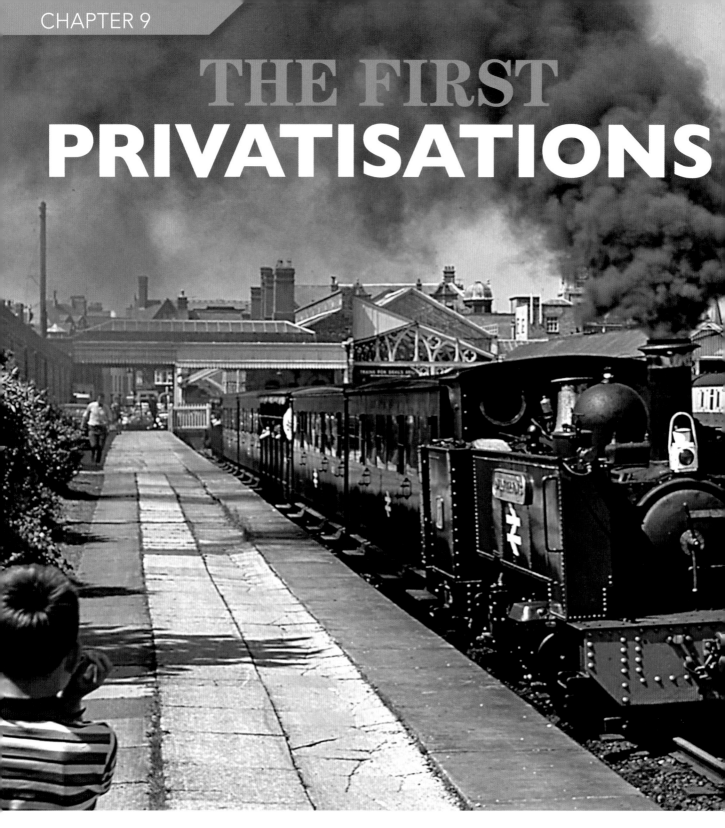

The operational heritage railway movement began in 1951 when, under the guidance of transport author Tom Rolt, the Talyllyn Railway was taken over by volunteers, many of which came from Birmingham and the West Midlands.

The Talyllyn milestone inspired The Titfield Thunderbolt, a 1953 Ealing comedy film about a group of villagers trying to keep their branch line operating after British Railways had decided to close it, and starred Stanley Holloway, George Relph and John Gregson. It was the first Ealing comedy shot in Technicolor.

Pure fiction, it planted the idea in the

consciousness of the British public that it was possible to save a railway line from being closed, and you did not have to accept everything that was dictated to you by those in power.

The headline-grabbing success of the Talyllyn initiative led to the takeover by volunteers of the moribund Ffestiniog Railway. However, neither of these lines had figured in the Grouping of 1923 nor Nationalisation 1948.

In 1959, the transport industry was rocked by the closure of a complete system within a system, the Midland & Great Northern Joint Railway network, which stretched from the East Midlands to the Norfolk coast. In October that

year, a pro-rail group, the Midland & Great Northern Joint Railway Society, was formed with the extremely over-ambitious plan to take over all 180 miles of the system and keep it running. History records that it never stood a chance.

However, 1960 saw the first two standard gauge heritage railways begin operations, in the form of the Middleton and Bluebell railways. There has always been a friendly debate as to which was the first to run heritage-era trains, but the Bluebell can claim an undisputed first.

It was the first heritage line to begin operations on a section of track, which

The heritage railway sector largely comprises lines that run on tracks that were once part of the nationalised network. However, two of them were sold in service to private operators.

Man bites dog: on April 5, 1969, the axe-wielding former British Railways' chairman Dr Richard Beeching officially reopened the branch from Buckfastleigh to Totnes as the Dart Valley Railway. SOUTH DEVON RAILWAY ARCHIVES

LEFT: The last bastion of British Rail steam was the Vale of Rheidol Railway, where the one-size-fits-all livery policy saw its fleet of three GWR 2-6-2Ts adorned in Rail Blue livery with the corporate double-arrow symbol. No. 7 *Owain Glyndwr* prepares to leave Aberystwyth station in 1970, while a main line diesel in matching livery, yellow front end apart, waits to depart with a Cambrian Coast Line service. COLOUR-RAIL

an extension of the M5 from Exeter. In the West Midlands, there were those who looked long and hard from a distance at the Bluebell achievement, and decided to do the same on their doorstep, ending up saving a section of the GWR Severn Valley cross-country route as the Severn Valley Railway.

In Yorkshire, local people tried to save the entire branch line from Keighley to Oxenhope again to retain community services, but ended up running a classic heritage line, the Keighley & Worth Valley Railway. It became a major visitor attraction boosted by the BBC and then EMI using it as the setting for film production of the immortal children's classic The Railway Children.

The lofty ambitions of those who formed the Midland & Great Northern Joint Railway Society in 1959 were drastically pruned back, and they ended up only with what was possibly the most scenic part of the closed system, that running from Sheringham to Weybourne and beyond, which became the North Norfolk Railway. Magnificent as these heritage lines became, in all of these instances it was a case of buying a disused line that British Railways had no intention of opening again, and was preparing to rip up the track.

However, there were two classic cases of sections of the nationalised network being bought in service from British Railways, with timetabled trains, at least at first, continuing to run as they did under state control, but under the auspices of a private operator.

had been acquired from British Railways following closure, in this case, the line from East Grinstead to Lewes.

At first, the Bluebell Railway Preservation Society leased a stretch of track from just south of Horsted Keynes. On August 7, 1960, the first Bluebell Railway services ran from Bluebell Halt, 100yds south of Horsted Keynes, to Sheffield Park.

In 1962, the society extended services to Horsted Keynes, and invited Dr Beeching to open a halt at Holywell (Waterworks). The halt closed within 12 months!

In the wake of the Bluebell success, revivalists elsewhere in the country

began to draw up plans to take over redundant lines. Many of them started out with the best intentions of running independent railways providing real public services, and ended up with a very different animal; a heritage line with purely seasonal and high days and holidays opening.

In the Sixties, the Dart Valley Railway was formed by businessmen to take over the moribund GWR Ashburton branch in South Devon as a money-making tourist attraction, but managed to save only the Totnes to Buckfastleigh section as the last length to Ashburton was taken by the Ministry of Transport for turning the A38 into a dual carriageway, effectively

A classic scene from the post-privatisation Paignton to Kingswear line, now marketed as the Dartmouth Steam Railway. GWR 2-6-2T No. 5239, named *Goliath* by the railway, heads south above the line of beach huts at Goodrington Sands. DSR

THE TORBAY TAKEOVER

The Dart Valley Railway made preservation history when it bought a second line in South Devon.

The single-track route from nearby Paignton to Kingswear, where it was linked to Dartmouth by ferry, was long regarded as a "main line by the back door", being an extension of the double-track line from Newton Abbot to Torquay and Paignton.

It was a route that was forever busy on summer Saturdays, in the days when many people still went on holiday by train rather than car.

While country branch lines were disappearing thick and fast both before and after the Beeching Axe, few ever thought that British Rail, as it was by then titled, would ever close any part of the branch. They were wrong.

The shock proposal to close the line south of Paignton came while Barbara Castle was Labour transport minister.

The line lost its Sunday trains from September 24, 1967, although some resumed during the summer of 1968. The crossing loop at Churston was closed on October 20, 1968 along with the updated signalbox at Kingswear.

The bombshell came in November 1968 when it was formally proposed that the line from Paignton to Kingswear should be closed entirely. But behind the scenes, a series of talks had begun. In 1972, Terry Holder a former director of The Economist became managing director of the Dart Valley Railway, and in the wake of the huge success of the Buckfastleigh operation, he saw enormous potential in the Kingswear line.

Multi-millionaire enthusiast, Sir William McAlpine, one of the early investors in the Dart Valley, who has a full-size standard gauge railway in the grounds of his home at Fawley Hill near Henley-on-Thames, paid BR £150 to hire a DMU to ride and inspect the Kingswear line. "This was a thing that could not be missed. It was a line which could take the very biggest locomotives, and we were worried that it would compete with the Buckfastleigh line."

Shock waves reverberated through the heritage sector when it was announced that Dart Valley Railway plc had, on December 30, 1972, bought the Paignton to Kingswear line. The news invited quips that the Dart Valley would next tender a bid to buy Paddington to Penzance!

Despite the takeover by a private company, the existing daily timetabled services continued without a break, from New Year's Day, 1973, with the Dart Valley Railway plc paying British Rail to run them.

The Paignton to Kingswear line had become the first operational passenger-carrying section of the national network to be denationalised, reversing the impact of 1948 if only on a little local basis.

The total purchase price of £275,000 included the whole line and most of the Kingswear waterfront including the Royal Dart Hotel. To recoup much of the purchase price the company subsequently sold off that and other surplus land assets.

However, to continue running 'ordinary' services as opposed to tourist or enthusiast trains quickly proved a bridge too far, as private companies would not benefit from the government subsidy of the national network.

Dart Valley Railway plc quickly found out that any profits from summer holiday season ticket sales were easily wiped out – and worse – by low patronage during the rest of the year, during which the extra seasonal carriages had to be stored.

So the operation of local trains all through the year by the line's new owner quickly came to an end after the first summer season. There would never be another winter timetable from Paignton to Kingswear, as the company from then on adopted the heritage/tourist attraction format of running only in profitable times of the year.

The line was rebranded as the Torbay Steam Railway and later the Paignton & Dartmouth Steam Railway. Today it is known simply as the Dartmouth Steam Railway, and it is the only UK heritage

PAIGNTON SOUTH DEVON

The beautiful panorama of Dartmouth's harbour, with Kingswear station in the foreground. DSR

line to pay dividends to its shareholders. Within a few years, the Paignton to Kingswear line upstaged the Dart Valley's original Buckfastleigh operation, which never improved on the 120,000 passengers carried in that first season, and by the late Eighties was seen as a drag on the company's resources.

The owning company then seriously considered closing the Buckfastleigh branch, however, its volunteer supporting body, the Dart Valley Railway Association, in 1990, took over the Buckfastleigh branch and ran it by itself, replacing paid staff wherever possible with volunteers.

The branch was rebranded as the South Devon Railway, and on February 8, 2010, the South Devon Railway bought its freehold and independence from Dart Valley Railway plc, for a nominal £1.

In GWR Brunswick green livery, Dartmouth Steam Railway flagship WR 4-6-0 No. 7827 *Lydham Manor* passes the wide sweep of Goodrington Sands en route to Churston and Kingswear. The stunning coastal scenery has made a major contribution to the success of this line, the first piece of British Rail to be privatised in that the line was sold in service to a private operator. DSR

RIGHT: Dartmouth Steam Railway flagship WR 4-6-0 No. 7827 *Lydham Manor* was built in 1950 and is a classic example of a Big Four design being built after Nationalisation before Robert Riddles launched his portfolio of Standard classes.

BELOW: While new operator Dart Valley Railway plc quickly found that a 365-days-a-year public service would never pay on the Paignton to Kingswear line that it bought in service from British Railways, it could profit from running trains outside Torbay's summer holiday season. On December 11, 2016, 1956-built BR Standard 4MT 4-6-0 No. 75014 – named *Braveheart* in preservation – passes Waterside with the 1.15pm Santa special to Kingswear. MARK WILKINS

SELLING OFF THE LAST BRITISH RAIL STEAM

The date of August 11, 1968, is always given as the end of British Rail steam, as it was on that date that the fabled 'Fifteen Guinea Special', pulled by four different steam locomotives in turn during the four legs of the journey, ran from Liverpool via Manchester to Carlisle and back, the day before a total ban on steam haulage over the network was imposed.

There was one exception to the ban: LNER A3 Pacific No 4472 *Flying Scotsman*, which in 1963 was sold out of service to Ffestiniog Railway saviour the late Alan Pegler, for the locomotive had previously booked commitments.

This did not spell the end of British Rail steam. For two decades afterwards, self-propelled steam cranes plied their trade over the network. Furthermore, one British Rail line continued to be hauled by steam locomotives inherited from the Great Western Railway.

As we saw earlier, British Railways inherited the Corris Railway from the GWR and closed it fairly quickly. Another narrow gauge line, coming within the Swindon portfolio, was the 2ft 6in gauge Welshpool & Llanfair Light Railway, which had lost its passenger services in 1931 and had been closed to freight in 1956.

It was reborn in 1963, after enthusiasts leased the track from British Railways, before buying it outright many years later. British Railways also had a third narrow gauge passed over from the GWR, in the Vale of Rheidol Railway running between Aberystwyth and Devil's Bridge in central Wales.

Uniquely, this railway was not made subject to the 1968 ban. Management at the London Midland Region saw the success that was being made at the revived Talyllyn and Ffestiniog railways, and decided that the Vale of Rheidol could similarly appeal to tourists, in an era when most UK holidaymakers still took their summer vacations in their own country.

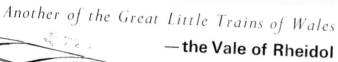

Another of the Great Little Trains of Wales
— the Vale of Rheidol

British Rail's only narrow-gauge line runs from Aberystwyth to Devil's Bridge through 12 miles of delightful scenery.

Trains run from Easter to the end of September.

Ask at Portmadoc Harbour Station or any British Rail office for details

The only steam on ☰☰ British Rail

LEFT: A 1970s British Rail advertisement for its only remaining steam line.

STEAM LOCOMOTIVES IN A DIESEL AND ELECTRIC LIVERY!

The scenic 11¾-mile Vale of Rheidol line, built by an independent company, opened on December 22, 1902 was formally taken over by the Cambrian Railways in 1913, and the latter became part of the GWR empire at the Grouping of 1923, with significant investment.

Three new 2-6-2Ts were built at Swindon in 1923: the new No. 7 and No. 8 were followed in 1924 by a 'refurbished' No. 2 *Prince of Wales*, which was in effect a new locomotive built from a third set of parts, described as a 'heavy overhaul' just to satisfy the GWR accountants, whereas the original No. 2 had been scrapped. Nos. 7 and 8 were named *Owain Glyndwr* and *Llywelyn* respectively in 1926. None of the original locomotives survived.

The GWR also built new passenger coaches to cater for the summer tourist traffic, eliminating the previous practice of carrying extra peak period passengers in freight wagons.

At Nationalisation, the line became part of the Western Region, and despite rumours of closure rumours in the mid-Fifties, it was transferred to the London Midland Region in 1963.

Following the highly unusual and eyebrow-raising decision by British Rail to keep the line running, despite the mass wave of closures of rural branch lines under the Beeching Axe throughout the rest of the country, the uniform Rail Blue corporate livery and double-arrow logo introduced by British Rail in 1964 were applied to the locomotives and carriages in 1967. Under the TOPS numbering arrangements for diesel and electric locomotives that was introduced by British Rail, the trio were designated Class 98 and nominally numbered 98007-98009, but they never carried these numbers.

The LMR soon regretted the decision to swim against the anti-steam tide and keep the line open. Partially because it was still run by paid staff rather than volunteers, as on the other surviving Welsh narrow gauge lines, losses mounted, and in 1967 British Rail made plans to close it. But, after a visit from Transport Minister Barbara Castle on July 1 of that year the little railway was reprieved.

In the Eighties, the Rail Blue livery gave way to more traditional liveries than the locomotives and stock had carried in the past, and afterwards British Rail's last steam line looked like any other heritage railway of the period.

On May 26, 1986, trackwork came apart at a curve near the 6½ mile post. A question was subsequently tabled in the House of Commons asking why British Rail was wasting its time on running a steam tourist line.

Two years later, British Rail decided to sell up. In April 1989, that Vale of

A diesel it certainly isn't, but nonetheless GWR 2-6-2T No. 7 *Owain Glyndwr* carries the British Rail corporate livery of main line locomotives in 1980. BARRY LEWIS*

Today's livery: No. 8 *Llywelyn* proudly wears its Great Western Railway maker's colours. The carriages are painted in matching chocolate and cream. Rail Blue is unlikely ever to return! BRIAN SHARPE

Rheidol Railway became the second privatisation of a state-owned line in regular passenger service.

It was bought by Tony Hills and Peter Rampton, owners of the Brecon Mountain Railway, a tourist line near Merthyr Tydfil.

In 1991, the Brecon partnership split, with Tony Hills keeping the Brecon line and Peter Rampton taking the Vale of Rheidol Railway. Eventually, the Vale of Rheidol Railway was transferred to the Phyllis Rampton Narrow Gauge Railway Trust, which is the line's major shareholder.

In 2000, the Railway Heritage Committee, a statutory body with the powers to 'claim' main line artefacts including rolling stock for preservation, designated the Vale of Rheidol Railway's three steam locomotives, 16 GWR bogie carriages, 11 four-wheel wagons and a guard's van. Under the designation, the items cannot be sold or scrapped without permission of the committee, the powers of which encompass any organisation that was once a subsidiary of British Rail.

Despite its privatisation, the Vale of Rheidol Railway still has the company registration number established by British Rail.

GWR livery for locomotives and rolling stock is the norm today, and current disdain for the line's BR Blue era is so great that its supporters would rather forget all about it.

RIGHT: In Rail Blue livery, No. 8 *Llywelyn* is seen at Pont ar Fynach in July 1984. VORR

CHAPTER 10

The break-up of British Rail

The election of a Conservative government that believed in free market enterprise and reducing burdens on the taxpayer led to British Rail being privatised in the Nineties – but it was far from a case of turning the clock back to 1947.

The winter of 1978-79 invited comparisons with that of 1962-63. Snow lay on the ground for several weeks and temperatures plummeted below zero over much of the country and stayed there. In addition, the country was hit by a wave of national strike action, often directed against the Labour government under Jim Callaghan, which would traditionally be on the side of the unions.

The whole package became known as the Winter of Discontent, and prompted a public backlash against those in power. On May 4, 1979, dawn broke to see a new party in government and a new prime minister the Conservative Margaret Thatcher.

Over the years, there had been a growing public feeling that state industries could be better run by private enterprise. There were many who believed that the costs to the taxpayer were too high, partially because there was an emphasis on keeping people in jobs for their own sake, and maintaining public sector wages artificially high.

To cut a long story short, the Thatcher government ushered in a wave

Prime Minister John Major, whose Conservative government authorised rail privatisation in 1993.

of privatisation of industries and sectors controlled by the state.

In the rail sector, rail-related businesses were sold off. The chain of British Transport Hotels was sold off, mainly one hotel at a time, between 1982-84, Sealink ferries by 1984, catering business Travellers Fare by 1988 and British Rail Engineering Ltd by 1989, not forgetting, of course, the Vale of Rheidol Railway.

In 1986, the possibility of breaking up British Rail was explored when discussions were held with Sea Containers concerning the possible takeover of the electric Ryde-Shanklin railway on the Isle of Wight.

The railway network as a whole was not privatised under Thatcher, but again, there was a wide belief that oversized rail subsidies were being unjustly borne by the taxpayer.

British Rail took a long hard look at itself in the late Eighties after being asked to reduce the amount of government subsidy, and reorganised itself on the basis of business sectors rather than geographical regions, a legacy from the Big Four days.

Firstly, in 1982, came Railfreight, the freight side of the business, followed in 1986 by InterCity, although the Inter-City brand had by then long been in operation.

A London & South East sector in 1986 became Network South East, while north of the border, services were transferred to ScotRail.

The existing regional management structure continued to work alongside the new sectors for some years before it was abolished.

On the whole, sectorisation was regarded within the rail industry as a great success, and paved the way for privatisation under Thatcher's successor John Major.

Hardcore Thatcherite Cecil Parkinson had advocated a privately or semi-privately operated rail network, but this was thought to be a privatisation too far by Thatcher, who won three elections in a row before standing down in 1990.

THE RAILWAYS ACT 1993

Opinion polls were never proved more wrong than in April 1992 when the Conservatives under John Major won that year's general election.

Rail privatisation was included in the party's manifesto for the election, but how it was to be accomplished was not specified.

After Major's surprise victory over Neil Kinnock's Labour, a plan by the Treasury, influenced by the Adam Smith Institute involved the creation of seven, later 25, passenger railway franchises as a way of maximising revenue.

In the biggest reversal since January 1, 1948, Britain's railways were privatised under the powers bestowed by the Railways Act 1993.

Its full title is, 'An Act to provide for the appointment and functions of a Rail Regulator and a Director of Passenger Rail Franchising and of users' consultative committees for the railway industry and for certain ferry services; to make new provision with respect to the provision of railway services and the persons by whom they are to be provided or who are to secure their provision; to make provision for and in connection with the grant and acquisition of rights over, and the disposal or other transfer and vesting of, any property, rights or liabilities by means of which railway services are, or are to be, provided; to amend the functions of the British Railways Board; to make provision with respect to the safety of railways and the protection of railway employees and members of the public from personal injury and other

Great North Eastern Railway was a Train Operating Company owned by Sea Containers, which following privatisation, operated the InterCity East Coast franchise from April 1996 until December 2007, when Sea Containers was stripped of the franchise owing to its financial management. It operated InterCity train services on the East Coast Main Line. One of its distinctive Class 2235 electric sets is seen approaching Greatford crossing in Lincolnshire on June 2, 2007. ROBIN JONES

risks arising from the construction or operation of railways; to make further provision with respect to transport police; to make provision with respect to certain railway pension schemes; to make provision for and in connection with the payment of grants and subsidies in connection with railways and in connection with the provision of facilities for freight haulage by inland waterway; to make provision in relation to tramways and other guided transport systems; and for connected purposes.'

Despite the term 'privatisation', there was no question of turning the clock back to December 31, 1947 and the days of the Big Four. For a start, many of the duplicated competing routes from the days of steam had long since been closed, and the national network had been significantly pared before, during and after Beeching.

Under the 1993 Act, the operations of the British Railway Board were broken up and sold off. The Act had been preceded on January 19 by the British Coal and British Rail (Transfer Proposals) Act, which was passed on January 19, 1993. It gave the secretary of state the power to issue directions to the British Railways Board to sell off assets, something the board had been unable to do until then.

British Rail's regulatory functions transferred to the newly created office of the Rail Regulator. Ownership of the infrastructure passed from April 1,

1994 to Railtrack, a group of companies that owned the track, signalling, tunnels, bridges, level crossings and most of the stations. Railtrack was floated on the Stock Exchange in May 1996.

Separately, track maintenance and renewal assets were sold to 13 companies across the network.

The ownership of British Rail's passenger trains passed to three rolling stock operating companies, with the stock in turn being leased out to passenger Train Operating Companies.

The TOCs were awarded contracts to run various routes and areas through a new system of rail franchising overseen by the Office of Passenger Rail Franchising.

With regards to British Rail's freight trains, their ownership and operation at first passed to two companies, English Welsh & Scottish Railway and Freightliner.

While private companies were placed in charge of much of the operation and assets of the former British Rail, it may still be held that a form of state control remained in place. For instance, a franchise holder that does not live up to expectations may have the franchise terminated early: that could never have happened in the Big Four of pre-Grouping eras.

EWS Class 37 No. 37419 at Bridgend with a service from Fishguard Harbour on June 26, 2004. PAUL SMITH

The crash scene near Hatfield after an InterCity 225 set derailed because of a cracked rail. CHRIS MILNER/THE RAILWAY MAGAZINE

THE ENDLESS DEBATE

Privatisation was a powder keg for political debate. There were those who claimed it had led to shareholders' interests being placed above those of the taxpayer and travelling public, and money, which could have been invested back into the network, was going to overseas companies.

The counter argument was that the taxpayer was asked to subsidise the railways less, there were lower fares and better traveller comfort and customer services through competition, and more investment in the railways.

The Labour party, grand architect of postwar nationalisation, took every opportunity to berate the Tory government over privatisation. Yet after Tony Blair took New Labour to a landslide victory in 1997, there was no attempt made to reverse the process. Labour went on to win two more terms

in office. Fatal accidents at Southall in 1997 and Ladbroke Grove in 1999 led to probing questions being asked about the dismemberment of the network under privatisation and its impact on both safety and maintenance procedures. Railtrack, which had a monopoly of infrastructure, was accused by both passenger interest groups and freight operators of not doing enough to maintain the network.

In February 1999, the company launched a bond issue that caused a significant fall in its share price, however, it was the Hatfield crash on October 17, 2000 that marked the beginning of the end for Railtrack.

The fatal accident on the East Coast Main Line in which four passengers died, was by no means one of the highest on the UK rail network in terms of loss of life. Yet its implication reached into every corner of the national network

and brought about the demise of the post-privatisation infrastructure-owning company that had succeeded British Rail.

A Great North Eastern Railway InterCity 225 set bound for Leeds with 170 passengers on board left King's Cross at 12.10pm on October 17, 2000.

It was travelling at 117mph when it became derailed south of Hatfield station 23 minutes later. The cause was a cracked rail. No. 91023, the leading Class 91 locomotive and the first two coaches did not derail but stayed upright. However, all those behind them including the Driving Van Trailer came off the tracks as the set split into three sections.

The eighth vehicle in the set was the restaurant car. It overturned on to its side and hit an overhead power line gantry, causing extensive damage. The four passengers who died in the crash were all in the restaurant car, and 70 more sustained injuries.

A preliminary investigation discovered that a rail had fragmented as trains passed and that the likely cause was, 'rolling contact fatigue' defined as multiple surface-breaking cracks. High loads cause such cracks where the wheels contact the rail. Repeated loading causes fatigue cracks to grow, and when they reach a critical size, the rail fails. More than 300 critical cracks were found in rails at Hatfield.

The problem was known about before the accident, and replacement rails had been made available, but had not been delivered to the correct location for installation.

Fears that other rails might be similarly affected meant that speed restrictions were imposed on huge lengths of track on the entire network, causing significant delays on many

A first Great Western Class 125 High Speed Train pulls into Totnes station next to Isambard Kingdom Brunel's atmospheric railway pumping station on September 13, 2009. First Great Western later rebranded itself as Great Western Railway. ROBIN JONES

routes, while checks were carried out. The number of cracks similar to those found at Hatfield throughout the UK was astonishing high.

Railtrack had hired maintenance contractors to do the maintenance work that had once been British Rail's responsibility, a strategy that left Railtrack bereft of adequate maintenance records and no accessible asset register.

The post-Hatfield delays caused profits by Train Operating Companies across the network to fall by 19% in the 12 months after the crash. Freight operator English, Welsh & Scottish Railway cancelled up to 400 trains per week as a result, while Freightliner's losses resulting from the delays were estimated at a £1-million per month.

In all, the cost to the national economy of the delays was estimated at £6 million per day.

In 2001, Railtrack announced that, despite making a pre-tax profit before exceptional expenses of £199 million, the £733 million of costs and compensation paid out over the Hatfield crash plunged Railtrack from profit to a loss of £534 million. It had to resort to approaching the government with a begging bowl, and then angered many by using the funding it received to pay a £137 million dividend to its shareholders in May 2001.

Railtrack's spiralling costs led to the collapse of the company, which entered administration at the insistence of Transport Secretary Stephen Byers MP, two years after Hatfield.

It was replaced under Byers' successor Alistair Darling MP by a not-for-dividend company that was in part state owned. Network Rail was formed with the principal purpose of acquiring and owning Railtrack plc, which it did on October 3, 2002. Railtrack plc was subsequently renamed Network Rail Infrastructure Limited, and so was effectively partially renationalised. At the time, groups that represented British train passengers welcomed the move.

AN EXPLOSION OF COLOUR!

Many observers, including myself, found the one-size-fits-all corporate blue livery of the British Rail years largely uninspiring and anodyne, but following privatisation liveries became a no-holds free-for-all with myriad candyfloss colours lighting up the network.

The private ownership of main line (as opposed to heritage) locomotives began in 1985 when the stone company Foster Yeoman bought a small number of extremely powerful 3600hp diesels from General Motors' Electromotive Division (GM-EMD) for use on mineral trains from its Somerset quarry. They were designated Class 59 by British Rail, whose staff manned them. They were so successful that quarry company ARC

Foster Yeoman Class 59/0 No. 59002 *Yeoman Enterprise* at Westbury on July 6, 1987. The quarry firm blazed a trail for the private ownership of main line locomotives years before privatisation. MICHAEL DAY*

and privatised power generator National Power also bought Class 59s to haul its trains. And this was before privatisation of the network!

The original three Rolling Stock Operating Companies continue to exist as originally established and have been joined by a variety of small-scale train owners ready to let old railway stock on short-term leases. Railtrack and its successor Network Rail have also purchased some rolling stock.

BACK UNDER STATE CONTROL

The grossly dismembered British Rail finally ceased to exist in 1997 but on two occasions, passenger franchises have had to be taken back, temporarily, into government ownership. The first was South Eastern Trains in 2003-2006, and East Coast in 2009-2015.

In addition, other government bodies have been given input into franchise terms; the Scottish government with ScotRail, the Welsh government in Wales & Borders, as well as the Mayor of London and regional passenger transport executives for the services in their respective areas.

Since 2005 the Department for Transport has been using the community railway designation to loosen the regulations and lower the costs and increase usage of selected socially necessary routes and services.

The regulatory structure has also evolved, in line with changes to the regulation of other privatised industries.

The position of Rail Regulator was abolished in 2004, and was replaced by a nine-member corporate board called the Office of Rail Regulation, incorporating responsibility for safety regulation, previously the remit of the Health and Safety Executive. It is now known as the Office of Rail & Road.

The calls for a complete renationalisation of the rail network a la 1948 were never to go away, and remain a perennial political debate.

There are those who assert that the Conservative dream of a shareholding nation by and large never came true, as most British company shares are owned by foreign investors, while it has been claimed that rail fares have risen by up to 25% in real terms since privatisation.

Back under state control: East Coast was a subsidiary of Directly Operated Railways, formed by the Department for Transport as an operator of last resort when National Express refused to provide further financial support to its National Express East Coast subsidiary and consequently lost its franchise for the East Coast Main Line in 2009. Two East Coast Class 91 electrics and two Class 125 High Speed Train sets are seen lined up at King's Cross on February 23, 2012. ROBIN JONES

CHAPTER 11

COULD CORBYN TURN THE STEEL WHEEL FULL CIRCLE?

The above-inflation rising cost of train tickets, strike action and below-par performances by franchise holders has led many, including Labour party leader Jeremy Corbyn, to ask, is it time to look at renationalising Britain's railways, 70 years on, *writes Bethany Edwards.*

For Jeremy Corbyn supporters, the election coverage on the morning of June 9, 2017 was a sight for tired eyes. Seasoned political commentators and Corbyn-sceptic MPs, prepped and primed for a landslide defeat, found themselves lost for words as it was revealed that Labour, a party polling at less than 30% when the snap election was called a few weeks previously had just generated the largest increase in the national vote share since Clement Atlee's government ascended to power in 1945, bringing us rail nationalisation in its wake.

This time round, safe seats, including one held by the Conservatives for 100 years, turned red overnight, while Tory heavyweights such as Amber Rudd and Justine Greening saw their majorities all but destroyed.

It didn't take long for the sceptics and BBC broadcasters to claim that no-one, not even them, could have seen such a political upheaval coming. But in arguing this, were they simply proving themselves to be just as short-sighted, and just as naïve as they had been in the run-up to the election?

While Corbyn's personal ratings remained dismal throughout the campaign, support for many policies put forward in Labour's For The Many manifesto appeared to be largely supported by the general public, with approval ratings for most policies continuing to soar afterwards.

Among the most popular policies were those centred around nationalisation, with targets including the Royal Mail, energy suppliers and the rail services.

Official portrait of Jeremy Corbyn. CHRIS ANDREW*

A Survation poll published in The Times found that support for nationalising industries is not only high, but far-reaching, with the majority supporting public ownership of water, electricity, gas, trains and defence. Half of those polled would support publicly owned banks; almost a quarter would be happy to see estate agents nationalised.

However, it's rail nationalisation that remains most popular with both Labour and Tory voters alike. Little wonder, given that today city bankers, public-sector workers and workers on zero-hour contracts are all equally reliant upon rail operators that, despite all the promises of improvements, continue to provide a quality of service that is frequently criticised as sub-standard, with steep rises in rail fares over the last decade only adding insult to injury.

While rail bosses have argued that the most recent hike announcement of 3.6% (starting the beginning of 2018) is in line with inflation, that will provide no comfort to those public-sector workers whose pay rises remain capped at 1%.

Those in favour of privatisation may naturally make the case that any additional expense, whether to cover inflation or pay for improvements, should only be borne by those in use of the service. Yet others argue that, in reality, this is a burden that falls upon every British taxpayer, regardless of their preferred mode of travel.

Reflecting upon the chaos of the Southern Rail strike in the summer of 2016, Guardian columnist Aditya Chakrabortty draws attention to an ideological inconsistency he regards as imperative to the continuation of

One of the modern Great Western Railway's new Class 800 electro-diesel Intercity Express Trains, No. 800008, at Reading on October 16, 2017, opposite InterCity Class 43 unit No. 43152, representative of a 40-year-old type that it will supersede. Built by Hitachi, the first units entered service on the Great Western Main Line in October 2017, and will debut with Virgin Trains on the East Coast Main Line from December 2018. However, 70 years after the formation of British Railways, Labour politicians are again arguing the case for nationalisation and bringing rolling stock and its owners, along with the track, under one roof once more. GWR

FOR THE MANY NOT THE FEW

THE LABOUR PARTY MANIFESTO 2017

Labour's 2017 general election manifesto, For The Many. The party was considered dead and buried at the spring local elections, but staged a remarkable 1945-style resurgence to deny Prime Minister Theresa May's Conservative party of a predicted 50-seat landslide and indeed her overall majority.

privatised rail: government subsidies. The flaws in this arrangement, he argues, have been exemplified no more devastatingly or embarrassingly than by Govia Thameslink Railway, which operates Southern.

GTR, Chakrabortty explains, "is unlike any other train company in Britain," in that it is paid billions by a government, "which then takes their ticket receipts and even refunds customers if the trains are delayed, effectively offering GTR no incentive for improving its services. Indeed, Southern's performance record does little to dispute this notion. Towards the end of last year, more than 35% of trains arrived at their destination more than five minutes late (the national average over the same period being 12.6%). The latest performance report

on the Gatwick Express website reveals a small degree of improvement: in the last week of September 2017, 22.2% of trains arrived more than five minutes late, yet still only 42.4% of Southern Mainline trains and 42.8% of Gatwick Express trains managed to arrive at the Right Time (within 50 seconds of the scheduled arrival time).

Another incongruity within this arrangement was made the focus of a video released by the transport union TSSA (Transport Salaried Staffs' Association) in early 2017. The video features ordinary citizens representing three European nations, France, Germany and the Netherlands, who all smugly thank the UK for keeping their rail services cheap, via profits made by state-backed European rail companies (the prime examples being German-

Southern Railway Class 313 EMU No. 313219 departs Portsmouth & Southsea with a West Coastway Line service for Brighton on September 6, 2013. In April 2016, Southern introduced a new method of door operation, with control of the doors moving from the conductor to the driver. Southern also proposed that, following the changes to the door operation, that conductors would now take on an "on-board supervisor role", which would enable them to be able to concentrate on the passengers more as opposed to the doors, but the National Union of Rail, Maritime and Transport Workers and ASLEF union described this as an attempt to make conductors unnecessary, which would also be unsafe. There followed a major industrial dispute resulting in the severe disruption and cancellation of Southern's trains, and during some strikes, temporarily shutting down the whole of the South East rail network in an attempt to stop the plans in their tracks. Prime Minister Theresa May and Secretary of State for Transport Chris Grayling, who labelled the strikes as appalling "and" palpable nonsense, led opposition to the strikes but in turn, the government came under fire for failing to act to resolve the situation. MATT BUCK*

owned Arriva, French state firm SCNF and Dutch state owned Abellio) operating on Network Rail.

After the left-wing, Labour-affiliated campaign group Momentum shared the video on its social media pages, a backlash came from many on the left, including some Labour MPs, who felt that key points – such as the stark difference in fare prices on privatised and nationalised railways – had been overshadowed by what many saw as xenophobic capitulating: the decision to pit foreign rail commuters and businesses against their British counterparts ("more Tory privatisation […] means we can take over even more") reminiscent of some of the more hard-right strains of the Leave campaign in 2015.

The video did not, however, explicitly blame the EU for the increased presence of European firms within the British Rail system, stating quite plainly that it is the current Conservative government that is spearheading further privatisation plans.

Another transport union, ASLEF, along with Labour MP Kate Hoey, took a slightly different stance during the run up to the referendum, citing the EU's 2012 Directive as a key factor influencing their decision to campaign for Leave. The EU directive is a policy that calls for "greater integration of the Union Transport sector" in order to "boost competition in railway service management". An expansion of the First Railway Directive, which enabled private companies to gain "non-

discriminatory" access to state-owned rail services.

Both Hoey and ASLEF argued that, if implemented, the policy could prove to be a considerable obstacle to any future attempts by Labour to fully renationalise Britain's railways.

Both unions, despite their differing positions concerning Britain's EU membership, do at least manage to highlight the somewhat inconsistent stance held by many Leave-backing Conservative MPs, including current leadership frontrunners Boris Johnson, Jacob Rees-Mogg and, the most recent entrant into the ring, the aptly named MP for Braintree James Cleverly.

During the referendum campaign, these MPs claimed it was time to "Take Back Control" of British laws, industries and jobs; arguing that British taxpayers' money would be better spent, not on remote European institutions, but on Britain's struggling public services. Yet these same politicians have voted consistently against both a publicly owned railway system and greater public control of bus services, allowing them instead to be sold off to European firms.

That these politicians continue to fail, or perhaps refuse, to recognise any disparity between such ideals and their party's own privatisation deals, could signal that the dream they have sold of a newly empowered, self-sufficient, post-Brexit Britain may well be just that –with little bearing on (and offering few answers to) the desperate, daily realities that have left so many clinging on to such a dream in the first place.

It may also explain why Labour, despite being led by some of the most unwavering pro-immigration politicians in both Labour and the UK's history, have found widespread, fresh support for their vision of a post-Brexit Britain.

In its 2017 manifesto, Labour announced the creation of what it described as 'The People's Railway', bringing the UK's railways back into public ownership either by simply taking back services once current contracts expire, by conducting franchise reviews, or taking advantage of break clauses present in some franchise contracts.

If Labour was to win the next general election, currently scheduled for May 2022, and if the current government does not allow any services to fall back into public ownership in the meantime, there would only be around half a dozen contracts expected to expire naturally during Labour's first term back in government.

It is not currently clear which (or even how many) contracts contain break clauses, and these could only be taken advantage of if a franchise's performance is considerably below expected standards, which could make the complete renationalisation of the railways, as a point of principle, a costly endeavour. This would also, of course, coincide with two other expensive, long-term rail projects: High Speed and Crossrail 2, which, collectively, look set to cost £85 billion, with neither expected to be finished before 2033.

While firmly opposed to Corbyn's renationalisation plans (dubbed by some Tory MPs as a "1970s idea") the Conservatives did also pay heed to the growing dissatisfaction among rail customers in their 2017 manifesto, proposing the introduction of a rail ombudsman to handle passenger complaints, and a review into rail ticketing services to remove 'complex and perverse' pricing. However, it is currently unclear when the Conservatives are planning to implement these proposals, or, given the overwhelmingly negative public reaction to the manifesto, whether these proposals will even be implemented at all.

A 'review' into ticket pricing also seems something of a back-step after the party's previous proposal to freeze all rail fares (in real terms) until 2020, as pledged in its 2015 manifesto. Not only do these proposals lack clarity and commitment (a criticism levelled at much of the manifesto) but the changes they could bring about seem incremental at best, especially compared with the radical, far-reaching ideas put forward in Labour's manifesto.

Since her party's disastrous faring at the election, Theresa May has admitted that the Conservatives' assumption over what comprises the 'political consensus', including ideas such as free-market economics, has been undermined by Corbyn, and that these arguments must now "be made all over again".

Chancellor Phillip Hammond, speaking to business leaders at the Conservative party conference, even went as far as to state that Corbyn poses "an existential challenge to our economic model" and that business should not "pull its punches in making the case for the market economy". But to win this argument, both the Conservatives and business leaders must defend the market economy's record in ways that reflect the interests and experiences of the majority (or "the many") – not in soundbites or hypotheticals, but with direct, concrete examples.

The argument, for example, that enabling competition in rail service management will result in higher levels of investment and greater scope for innovation (resulting in improved standards) could be exemplified by the recent takeover of South West Trains (now South Western Railway) by FirstGroup – which pledged £1.2-billion of investment to pay for 90 new trains, station improvements and refurbished carriages including free wifi and air conditioning.

However, publicising such a case could result in increased scrutiny of concerns raised by those opposing the takeover. After FirstGroup was awarded the SWT contract, the Competition and Markets Authority pointed out that this now meant the firm would have control of services to Exeter on both the South Western and Great Western franchises, reducing competition on the route, and thus allowing FirstGroup to increase fares for passengers between London and Exeter.

Existing South West Trains' customers have also expressed anger over fast-route morning services being cut as a result of the takeover, which has led to even some Conservative MPs, such as the representative for North East Hampshire, Ranil Jayawardena, promoting petitions calling for the repeal of cuts to local rail services. In effect, FirstGroup is attempting to attract more customers with promises of a better-quality service, while simultaneously reducing capacity on services not only for new customers, but

A post-Beeching closure was rolled back on June 13, when 'real' – as opposed to enthusiast or tourist services – began running the full length of Dorset's Swanage branch for the first time since British Rail closed in on January 1, 1972. Fifty years after the end of Southern steam, passenger services are running again over the entire length of one of the fabled seaside branch lines, which served the south coast.

The Swanage branch closed – nobody appears to know exactly why – on January 1, 1972. Around 500 passengers made the last return trip on a six-coach train, comprising two 1957-built Hampshire DEMUs.

Enthusiasts spent more than four decades rebuilding the branch and restoring it as the heritage Swanage Railway, with the ultimate ambition of restoring public services from the Purbeck resort to Wareham. Long hailed as a perfect microcosm of the Southern Railway/Region as it was in the days of steam, it was diesels provided by market-leading heritage main line operator West Coast Railways of Carnforth, Lancashire, that hauled the ground-breaking services, being run on selected days for a two-year trial period and funded by government and local council grant aid.

West Coast Railways' maroon-livered Class 37 diesel No. 37518 is pictured standing alongside one of Robert Riddles' BR Standard 4MT 2-6-4Ts at Corfe Castle; the ruins of which give the picture-postcard Purbeck stone village

its name. Marking 50 years since the end of Southern Region steam No. 80104 has been given the identity of scrapped sister No. 80146, which ran on the Swanage branch in 1967. If the Swanage-Wareham trial proves a success, in this age of worsening road congestion, might other seaside branch lines be similarly reopened, in a modern-day reversal of rail fortunes? ANDREW PM WRIGHT

On October 28, 2015, Class 91 electric No. 91132 was named *Flying Scotsman* by Scottish First Minister Nicola Sturgeon, celebrating one of the most famous names in railway history. She said: "For over 150 years the 'Flying Scotsman' service has connected Edinburgh and London by the historic East Coast rail route. It is wonderful to see the name of the 'Flying Scotsman' train kept alive on the route with a new, contemporary design." Virgin, which runs services on both the East and West Coast main lines, has long been hailed as one of the major success stories of rail privatisation. VIRGIN TRAINS

for those already using these services, many without any other alternative.

Overcrowding became a hotly contested issue during the summer of 2016, following the release of video, published on the Guardian's website, showing Labour leader Jeremy Corbyn sitting on the floor of a carriage after apparently failing to find a seat on a packed Virgin train. Corbyn framed this predicament as being a culmination of the failings of private rail companies, stating that: "the reality is there are not enough trains – we need more of them, they're also very expensive" before concluding, "Isn't that a good case for public ownership?".

The video prompted hundreds of exasperated Virgin train customers to flood social media with anecdotes, stories and photographic evidence of the poor conditions they are regularly forced to endure on Virgin rail services.

It didn't take long, however, for Richard Branson to launch a virulent defence of the service, posting CCTV images on his Twitter account of Corbyn walking past several apparently vacant seats before choosing to sit on the floor. Despite many on social media claiming to have experienced similar conditions on Virgin trains, for Corbyn, the damage was done, with accusations of dishonesty levelled at a leader previously heralded (even by some naysayers) as a straight-talking man of principle.

Months after the dust had settled, new footage emerged of the same seats with clearly visible reserved tickets, some even occupied by largely obscured passengers. Not only were the initial images posted by Branson apparently misrepresentative, but concerns have since been raised regarding the company's decision to publish CCTV footage featuring ordinary passengers, with the Information Commissioner's Office ruling that Virgin "had breached the data protection rights" of ordinary passengers on the train.

The transparency and accountability of private firms operating within public services is an issue that has come under increased scrutiny in the last year, particularly concerning public health and safety. Both NHS workers and rail workers have gone on strike over safety concerns, which have been consistently dismissed by government departments and (in the case of the railways), private companies alike.

A feeling of palpable distrust is growing, informed by the idea – crystallized in the minds of many during the aftermath of Grenfell Tower – that the Conservatives' alliance with large, private firms is one rooted in self-interest, and increasingly at the expense of the public. This is a profound problem for the Tories, of the kind that can't be resolved by a catchy soundbite or a new lick of paint.

Britain's railways are just one example of an area where Labour seems to be far more in tune with the majority of the British public than the current government. If the Conservatives wish to rectify this and remain in power, they must begin to develop a vision for Britain, which is as radical, transformative and far-reaching as that put forward by Labour, with the needs and interests of the British public at its heart and centre.

Services like the railways must no longer be regarded as commodities, while members of the public must feel like more than just customers.

Since becoming leader of the Labour party in 2015, Jeremy Corbyn has often publicly divulged – one suspects, to much hilarity among the Conservatives' PR team – his many niche interests, including jam-making, allotments, drain covers… and trains. In an interview with Lorraine Kelly broadcast shortly after becoming leader, Corbyn confessed that, when travelling up and down the country, "whoever is travelling with me gets more information [about the railways] than they probably need."

On reflection, perhaps this personal (as opposed to profit-driven) investment in, and genuine passion for Britain's railways, could be exactly what British rail needs to become, once again. A source of national pride, that Britons of any political persuasion can enjoy.

Maybe it's time for January 1, 1948, all over again.